KEY CASES

CRIMINAL LAW

JACQUELINE MARTIN

GW00497566

Hodder Arnold

A MEMBER OF THE HODDER HEADLINE GROUP

Orders: please contact Bookpoint Ltd, 130 Milton Park, Abingdon, Oxon OX14
4SB. Telephone: (44) 01235 827720. Fax: (44) 01235 400454. Lines are open from
9.00 – 6.00, Monday to Saturday, with a 24 hour message answering service.
You can also order through our website www.hoddereducation.co.uk

If you have any comments to make about this, or any of our other titles, please send
them to educationenquiries@hodder.co.uk

British Library Cataloguing in Publication Data
A catalogue record for this title is available from the British Library

ISBN-10: 0 340 91501 3
ISBN-13: 978 0 340 915011

This edition published 2006
Impression number   10 9 8 7 6 5 4 3 2
Year   2008 2007 2006

Hodder Headline's policy is to use papers that are natural, renewable and recyclable
products and made fromwood grown in sustainable forests. The logging and
manufacturing processes are expected to conform to the environmental regulations
of the country of origin.

Typeset by Transet Limited, Coventry, England.
Printed in Great Britain for Hodder Arnold, an imprint of Hodder Education, a
member of the Hodder Headline Group, 338 Euston Road, London NW1 3BH by
Cox & Wyman Ltd., Reading, Berkshire.

CONTENTS

Chapter 6 INCHOATE OFFENCES

Chapter 7 CAPACITY

Chapter 8 INSANITY, AUTOMATISM AND INTOXICATION

Chapter 9 DURESS AND NECESSITY

Chapter 10 MISTAKE, SELF-DEFENCE, CONSENT

Chapter 11 HOMICIDE

Chapter 12 ASSAULTS

Chapter 18 PUBLIC ORDER OFFENCES

TABLE OF CASES

PREFACE

The Key Cases series is designed to give a clear understanding of important cases. This is useful when studying a new topic and invaluable as a revision aid.

Each case is broken down into fact and law. In addition, many cases are extended by the use of important extracts from the judgment or by comment or by highlighting problems. In some instances students are reminded that there is a link to other cases or material. If the link case is in another part of the same Key Cases book, the reference will be clearly shown. Some links will be to additional cases or materials that do not feature in the book.

To give a clear layout, symbols have been used at the start of each component of the case. The symbols are:

 Key Facts – These are the basic facts of the case.

 Key Law – This is the major principle of law in the case, the *ratio decidendi*.

 Key Judgment – This is an actual extract from a judgment made on the case.

 Key Comment – Comments made on the case.

 Key Problem – Apparent inconsistencies or difficulties in the law.

 Key Link – This indicates other cases in the text that should be considered in conjunction with this case.

At the start of each chapter there are mind maps highlighting the main cases and points of law. In addition, within most chapters, one or two of the most important cases are boxed to identify them and stress their importance.

Each Key Case book can be used in conjunction with the Key Facts book on the same subject. Equally, they can be used as additional material to support any other textbook.

This Key Case book on criminal law starts with cases on general principles and then covers the main areas of offences against the person, offences against property and offences against public order. The law is stated as I believe it to be on 1st February 2006.

Jacqueline Martin

CHAPTER 1

INTRODUCTION TO CRIMINAL LAW

PURPOSE OF LAW

Brown (1993)
The law should protect society from a cult of violence

Wilson (1996)
Consensual marital behaviour was not criminal BUT the law should develop on a case by case basis

JUDICIAL LAW-MAKING

Shaw v DPP (1961)
Created the offence of corrupting public morals
Knuller v DPP (1973)
Recognised that *Shaw* had created the offence of corrupting public morals: majority also thought an offence of outraging public decency existed
R (1991)
Law should change with society

INTRODUCTORY POINTS

ELEMENTS OF A CRIME

Fagan v MPC (1968)
Actus reus can be a continuing act, so that if *mens rea* is superimposed on it at any point it completes the offence

Thabo Meli v R (1954)
Where *mens rea* and *actus reus* are present in a series of acts then there is sufficient coincidence for D to be guilty

BURDEN OF PROOF

Woolmington (1935)
Where D raises a defence it is for the prosecution to negate that defence
This applies to nearly all defences

Lambert (2001)
It is normally a breach of human rights for D to have to prove innocence

Sheldrake (2004)
BUT imposing a legal burden of proof on D is not objectionable where the offence carries risk of death and the relevant information is within D's knowledge

1.1 Purpose of law

HL *Brown* [1993] 2 All ER 75, (1993) 97 Cr App R 44

 Five men in a group of consenting adult sado-masochists were convicted of offences of assault causing actual bodily harm (s 47 Offences Against the Person Act 1861) and malicious wounding (s 20 Offences Against the Person Act 1861). They had carried out acts which included applying stinging nettles to the genital area and inserting map pins or fish hooks into each other's penises. All the victims had consented and none had needed medical attention.

 Consent could not be used as a defence to charges of assault, even though the acts were between adults in private and did not result in serious bodily injury.

 Lord Templeman
'Society is entitled and bound to protect itself against a cult of violence. Pleasure derived from the infliction of pain is an evil thing. Cruelty is uncivilised'.

 Two of the judges in the House of Lords dissented in this case. Lord Mustill thought that the case raised 'questions of private morality' and that the standards by which the defendants should be judged were not those of the criminal law. This dissent among the judges shows the difficulty of deciding just when the judges should intervene. Compare the decision with that in the next case.

Wilson [1996] 3 WLR 125, [1996] 2 Cr App R 241

A husband had used a heated butter knife to brand his initials on his wife's buttocks, at her request. The wife's burns became infected and she needed medical treatment. He was convicted of assault causing actual bodily harm (s 47 Offences Against the Person Act 1861) but on appeal the Court of Appeal quashed the conviction.

Consent was a defence in such a case. However, the law should develop on a case-by-case basis.

Russell LJ
'It is not in the public interest that activities such as the appellant's in this appeal should amount to a criminal behaviour. Consensual activity between husband and wife, in the privacy of the matrimonial home, is not, in our judgment, a proper matter for criminal investigation, let alone criminal prosecution'.

Attorney-General's Reference (No 6 of 1980) [1981] 2 All ER 1057.

See **8.8**.

1.2 Judicial law-making

HL *Shaw v DPP* [1962] AC 220, (1961) 45 Cr App R 113

D published a directory of prostitutes. It included photographs of some of the prostitutes and information on the type of conduct in which they were prepared to participate.

The House of Lords created the offence of conspiracy to corrupt public morals as there did not appear to be an offence which covered the situation.

Viscount Simmonds
'I entertain no doubt that there remains in the courts a residual power to enforce the supreme and fundamental purpose of the law, to conserve not only the safety and order but also the moral welfare of the state …'.

This case highlights whether unelected judges should make law. It can be argued that if Parliament has chosen not to prohibit certain conduct then it is not for judges to fill the gaps.

 Knuller (Publishing, Printing and Promotions) Ltd v DPP
[1973] AC 435, (1972) 56 Cr App R 633

The appellants published a magazine which contained, on inside pages, a number of advertisements headed 'Males'. Most of these were put in by homosexuals with the intention of meeting other men for homosexual purposes. At the time, the age of consent for homosexual behaviour was 21. The appellants accepted that many males under the age of 21 would see the advertisements and that some of them might reply.

The appellants were charged with (1) conspiracy to corrupt public morals and (2) conspiracy to outrage public decency. They were convicted of both charges and appealed.

The offence of corrupting public morals existed. It had been created in *Shaw v DPP* (1962) and it was for Parliament, not the courts, to abolish it. The appellants' conviction for (1) was upheld. However, the appellants' conviction for (2) was quashed.

The judges were divided as to whether an offence of outraging public decency existed. Two of them held that it did not and that the courts could not create such an offence. The other three held that such an offence did exist, but quashed the conviction because the trial judge had not directed the jury adequately on what was meant by 'outrage'.

The existence of the offences of corrupting public morals and outraging public decency has been recognised by Parliament in the Criminal Law Act 1977. Section 5(1) of this Act abolished common law conspiracy, but s 5(3)(a) specifically provides that the offences of conspiracy to corrupt public morals with conspiracy to outrage public decency were not abolished.

HL *R* [1991] 4 All ER 481, (1991) 94 Cr App R 216

D and his wife had separated and agreed to seek a divorce. Three weeks later, D broke into the wife's parents' home, where she was staying, and attempted to rape her.

Although old authorities stated that a man could not be guilty of raping his wife, the law had to evolve to suit modern society. D could be guilty.

Lord Keith of Kinkel
'[The] question is whether … this is a an area where the court should step aside to leave the matter to the parliamentary process. This is not the creation of a new offence, it is the removal of a common law fiction which has become anachronistic and offensive and we consider that it is our duty, having reached that conclusion, to act upon it'.

D took the case to the European Court of Human Rights, claiming that the retrospective recognition of martial rape was a breach of Article 7 of the European Convention on Human Rights. It was held that there was no breach of Article 7. In fact, abandoning the idea that a husband could not be prosecuted for rape of his wife conformed with the fundamental objective of respect for human dignity.

1.3 Elements of a crime

 Fagan v Metropolitan Police Commissioner
[1968] 3 All ER 442, (1968) 52 Cr App R 700

D accidentally drove his car onto a police officer's foot. When D was asked to move the car, he refused to do so for some time. He was convicted of assaulting a police officer in the execution of his duty. This involved proving an assault.

The *actus reus* of assault could be a continuing act so that if D developed the necessary *mens rea* at any time during that period, he could be guilty of battery.

James J

'For an assault to be committed, both the elements of *actus reus* and *mens rea* must be present at the same time ... It is not necessary that *mens rea* should be present at the inception of the *actus reus*, it can be superimposed on an existing act. On the other hand, the subsequent inception of *mens rea* cannot convert an act which has been completed without *mens rea* into an assault'.

Would the failure of D to remove his car from the police officer's foot now be recognised as the *actus reus* of assault? This would be in line with the decision in *DPP v Santa-Bermudez* [2003] EWHC 2908, where D's failure to tell a police woman that there was a needle in his pocket which she was about to search was held to be sufficient for the *actus reus* of assault. (See **12.1.1**.)

Thabo Meli v R [1954] 1 All ER 373

Ds attacked a man and believed they had killed him. They then pushed his body over a low cliff. In fact, the man had survived the attack and died of exposure when unconscious at the foot of the cliff.

Provided that the required *mens rea* and *actus reus* were combined in a series of acts, a defendant could be guilty.

- *Church* [1965] 2 All ER 72, (1965) 49 Cr App R 206 (see **11.4**);
- *Le Brun* [1991] 4 All ER 673, (1991) 94 Cr App R 101 (see **11.4**).

1.4 Burden of proof

CT **Woolmington v DPP**
[1935] AC 462, (1935) 25 Cr App R 72

D went to ask his wife to return to him. He took with him a loaded sawn-off shotgun with which, he claimed, he intended to commit suicide if she refused to return to him. Following her refusal, he brought the gun out from under his coat, to show her he meant to commit suicide. As he brought it across his waist it somehow went off, killing his wife. He claimed that this was a pure accident.

When D raises a defence, it is for the prosecution to negate that defence. This is part of the prosecution's duty to prove D's guilt.

Lord Sankey
'Throughout the web of the English criminal law one golden thread is always to be seen – that it is that duty of the prosecution to prove the prisoner's guilt ... No matter what the charge or where the trial, the principle that the prosecution must prove the guilt of the prisoner is part of the common law of England and no attempt to whittle it down can be entertained'.

HL *Lambert* [2001] UKHL 37, [2001] 2 Cr App R 511

This concerned s 28(2) of the Misuse of Drugs Act 1971 which states that a defendant shall be acquitted if he 'proves that he neither believed nor suspected nor had any reasons to suspect that the substance or product in question was a controlled drug'. D claimed that this subsection meant he had to prove his innocence and this was a breach of Article 6(2) of the European Convention on Human Rights (the presumption of innocence). The appeal failed because a majority of the Lords held that the Human Rights Act 1998 was not retrospective.

A majority of the Law Lords held that if s 28(2) of the Misuse of Drugs Act 1971 was read as imposing a legal burden on the defendant to prove lack of knowledge, then this undermined the presumption of innocence to an impermissible extent. However, they thought it could be read down as imposing only an evidential burden. They did this by interpreting the subsection as meaning not 'prove' but 'introduce evidence of'.

Is this interpretation of the subsection really viable? The word used in it is 'prove'. This idea of 'reading down' so as to impose an evidential burden rather than a legal one was also used in *Attorney-General's Reference (No 4 of 2002)* (2004), which was heard together with the appeal in *Sheldrake* (2004) (see below).

Sheldrake v DPP [2004] UKHL 43

Sheldrake was convicted of being in charge of a motor car in a public place after consuming so much alcohol that he exceeded the prescribed limit, contrary to s 5(1)(b) of the Road Traffic Act 1988. He appealed to the Divisional Court who allowed his appeal. The prosecution appealed to the House of Lords.

The defence argued that s 5(2) infringed the presumption of innocence guaranteed by Article 6(2) as it imposed on the defendant a legal burden of proving innocence by proving a defence. The House of Lords allowed the prosecution's appeal and reinstated the conviction.

The House of Lords held that s 5(2) did impose a legal burden of proof on the defendant but it was justified.

Lord Bingham

'It is not objectionable to criminalise a defendant's conduct in these circumstances without requiring a prosecutor to prove criminal intent. The defendant has a full opportunity to show that there was no likelihood of his driving, a matter so closely conditioned by his own knowledge … as to make it much more appropriate for him to prove, on the balance of probabilities, that he would not have been likely to drive than for the prosecutor to prove beyond reasonable doubt that he would'.

CHAPTER 2

ACTUS REUS

OMISSIONS AS *ACTUS REUS*
This can occur where D owes a duty of care
***Gibbins and Proctor* (1918)**
Parents and anyone who has undertaken the care of a child owe a duty to that child
***Stone and Dobinson* (1977)**
D may owe a duty to vulnerable family members. Anyone undertaking care of an elderly person may owe a duty
***Miller* (1983)**
Where D sets in motion a chain of events which might cause harm, he has a duty of care
***Dytham* (1979)**
There may be a duty because of a public office

CAUSATION
***White* (1910)**
The act must be the factual cause

***Pagett* (1983)**
A reasonable response in self defence does not break the chain of causation

***Malcherek* (1981)**
Switching off a life-support machine does not break the chain of causation

***Cheshire* (1991)**
Negligent treatment by medical staff does not normally break the chain of causation

ACTUS REUS

INTERVENING ACTS
***Roberts* (1972)**
Where V's intervening act is reasonably foreseeable then it does not break the chain of causation

***Williams and Davis* (1992)**
If V's conduct is not reasonably foreseeable then it will break the chain of causation

2.1 Liability for omissions

 Gibbins and Proctor (1918) 13 Cr App R 134

Gibbins and his partner starved his seven-year-old daughter to death. The other children of the family were well cared for and fed.

An omission can be the *actus reus* of murder where a duty exists. In this case Gibbins, as the child's father, had a duty towards her. His partner had undertaken care of the children and so also owed a duty to the child.

 Stone and Dobinson [1977] QB 354, (1977) 64 Cr App R 186

Stone's sister, Fanny, came to live with the defendants. Fanny was eccentric and often stayed in her room for several days. She also failed to eat. She eventually became bed-ridden and incapable of caring for herself. On at least one occasion Dobinson helped to wash Fanny and also occasionally prepared food for her. Fanny died from malnutrition. Both Ds were found guilty of her manslaughter.

As Fanny was Stone's sister he owed a duty of care to her. Dobinson had undertaken some care of Fanny and so also owed a duty of care. The duty was to either help her themselves or to summon help from other sources. Their failure to do either of these meant that they were in breach of their duty.

Dytham [1979] QB 722

D was a police officer who was on duty. V was ejected from a nightclub about 30 yards from where D was standing. There was a fight and three men kicked V to death. D took no steps to intervene or summon help. When the fight was over, D told a bystander he was going off duty and left the scene. He was convicted of misconduct in a public office.

An omission (a wilful failure to act) was sufficient for the *actus reus*. D had a duty to protect V or to arrest the attackers or otherwise bring them to justice.

 Miller [1983] 1 All ER 978, (1983) 77 Cr App R 17

D was living in a squat. He fell asleep while smoking a cigarette. He awoke to find his mattress on fire. He went into another room and went back to sleep. The house caught fire. He was convicted of arson.

Where D had set a chain of events in motion which might cause harm, a failure to take reasonable steps to deal with the fire when he discovered his mattress was on fire meant that he had committed the *actus reus* for arson.

DPP v Santa-Bermudez [2003] EWHC 2908 (see **12.1.1**).

2.2 Causation

 White [1910] 2 KB 124, (1910) 4 Cr App R 257

D added poison to his mother's drink, with the intention of killing her. The evidence showed she died of a heart attack but there was no evidence to show she had drunk any of the poison. Also, the amount of poison was insufficient to kill her in any event.

Although D had the intention to kill and did the act of putting poison into his mother's drink, his act was not the cause of her death so that he could not be guilty of murder.

Attempts – see **6.3**.

 Pagett [1983] Crim LR 393, (1983) 76 Cr App R 279

D took his girlfriend, who was pregnant by him, from her home by force. He then held the girl hostage. Police called on him to surrender. D came out, holding the girl in front of him and firing at the police. The police returned fire and the girl was killed by police bullets. D was convicted of manslaughter.

(1) D's act need not be the sole cause, nor need it be the main cause. It is enough if his act contributed significantly to the death.
(2) A reasonable act in self-defence caused by D's own acts is not an intervening act for the purpose of breaking the chain of causation.

Goff LJ
'There can, we consider, be no doubt that a reasonable act performed for the purpose of self-preservation, being of course an act caused by the accused's own act, does not operate as a *novus actus interveniens*'.

 Malcherek **[1981] 2 All ER 422, (1981) 73 Cr App R 173**

D stabbed his wife in the stomach. At hospital, she was put on a life-support machine. After a number of tests showed that she was brain dead, the machine was switched off. D was charged with her murder. The trial judge refused to allow the issue of causation to go to the jury. D was convicted. He appealed.

Discontinuance of treatment by switching off a life-support machine does not break the chain of causation. The original attacker is still liable for the death.

CA *Cheshire* **[1991] 3 All ER 670, [1991] Crim LR 709**

D shot V in the stomach. V was treated in hospital where a tracheotomy tube was inserted to help him breathe. Two months later, when his wounds were virtually healed, V died of a rare complication caused by the tracheotomy.

D's acts need not be the sole cause or even the main cause of death. It is sufficient if his acts contributed significantly to the death. Negligent treatment by medical staff will not normally exclude D's responsibility for the death

Beldam LJ

'Even though negligence in the treatment of the victim was the immediate cause of death, the jury should not regard it as excluding the responsibility of the accused unless the negligent treatment was so independent of his acts, and in itself so potent in causing death, that they regard the contribution made by his acts as insignificant.'

The level of negligence in medical treatment required to break the chain of causation is very high – 'so potent in causing death'. It will only be in an exceptional case that medical treatment will break the chain of causation. The courts are likely to hold the original attacker liable for the death even where the medical treatment is 'thoroughly bad' (*Smith* (1959))

- *Smith* [1959] 2 QB 35 Courts Martial Appeal Court;
- *Jordan* (1956) 40 Cr App R 152 CA;
- *Mellor* [1996] 2 Cr App R 245 CA.

 Roberts [1972] Crim LR 27, (1971) 56 Cr App R 95

V was a passenger in D's car. While driving along, D made sexual advances to V and attempted to pull her coat off. She jumped from the car and was injured. D was convicted of an assault occasioning actual bodily harm.

A foreseeable act by V does not break the chain of causation.

Stephenson LJ

'The test is: Was it a natural result of what the alleged assailant said and did, in the sense that it was something that could reasonably have been foreseen as the consequence of what he was saying or doing?'

 Williams and Davis [1992] 2 All ER 183, (1992) 95 Cr App R 1

Ds gave a lift to a hitch-hiker. He (V) jumped from Ds' car when it was travelling at about 30 mph, allegedly because Ds had tried to rob him. V died from head injuries. Both Ds were convicted of manslaughter. The Court of Appeal quashed their convictions.

V's conduct must be something which could be reasonably foreseen. If it is not reasonably foreseeable then the chain of causation is broken.

Stuart-Smith LJ

'There must be some proportionality between the gravity of the threat and the action of the deceased in seeking to escape from it … [T]he deceased's conduct … [must] be something that a reasonable and responsible man in the assailant's shoes would have foreseen … [T]he nature of the threat is of importance in considering both the foreseeability of harm to the victim from the threat and the question whether the deceased's conduct was proportionate to the threat, that is to say that it was within the ambit of reasonableness and not so daft as to make it his own voluntary act which amounted to a *novus actus interveniens* and consequently broke the chain of causation'.

CHAPTER 3

MENS REA

INTENTION
Mohan (1975)
Intention is a decision to bring about a certain consequence
Moloney (1985)
Foresight of consequences is evidence of intention
Hancock and Shankland (1986)
Probability is important in foresight of consequences
Nedrick (1986)
The conseqence has to be a virtual certainty and D must realise this
Woollin (1998)
Where the consequence is a virtual certainty and D realises this, the jury can *find* intention

RECKLESSNESS
Cunningham (1957)
Maliciously means either intention or subjective recklessness
Caldwell (1981)
This case created objective recklessness, where D could be guilty if the risk would have been obvious to an ordinary prudent person
G and another (2003)
This case overruled *Caldwell*. Recklessness means that D must realise there is risk and take that risk

MENS REA

GROSS NEGLIGENCE
Bateman (1925)
The negligence must be higher than for a civil case. D's conduct must show such disregard for the life and safety of others as to amount to a crime

Adomako (1994)
The three elements of negligence must be present AND the breach must be sufficiently serious to make it criminal

TRANSFERRED MALICE
Latimer (1886)
An intention can be transferred to an unintended victim

Pembliton (1874)
Malice cannot be transferred if D intended a completely different offence

A-G's ref (No 3 of 1994) (1997)
Confirmed that the doctrine of transferred malice is good law

3.1 Intention

PC **Mohan** [1975] 2 All ER 193, (1975) 60 Cr App R 272

In order to get away, D drove his car at a police officer. The officer jumped out of the way and was not injured. D was convicted of attempting to cause bodily harm to a police officer by wanton driving.

Intention is not the same as motive. Intention is a decision to bring about a certain consequence.

HL **Moloney** [1985] 1 All ER 1025, (1985) 81 Cr App R 93

D and his stepfather had drunk a considerable amount at a family party. After the party they were heard talking and laughing. Then there was a shot. D phoned the police, saying he had just murdered his father. D said that they had been seeing who was the fastest at loading and firing a shotgun. He had loaded his gun the fastest. His stepfather then said he hadn't 'got the guts' to pull the trigger. D said 'I didn't aim the gun. I just pulled the trigger and he was dead'.

Foresight of consequences is evidence of intention.

Lord Bridge
'I am firmly of the opinion that foresight of consequences, as an element bearing on the issue of intention in murder, or

indeed any other crime of specific intent, belongs not to the substantive law but to the law of evidence'.

Lord Bridge in his judgment in *Moloney* discussed s 8 of the Criminal Justice Act 1967 but finished by giving guidelines on the question of foresight of consequences which did not use the word 'probable' which is used in the section. He referred only to a natural result. This omission of the word 'probable' was held in *Hancock and Shankland* (1986) (see below) to make the guidelines defective.

HL | *Hancock and Shankland* [1986] 1 All ER 641, (1986) 82 Cr App R 264

Ds were miners who were on strike. They tried to prevent another miner from going to work by pushing a concrete block from a bridge onto the road along which he was being driven to work in a taxi. The block struck the windscreen of the taxi and killed the driver. The trial judge used the *Moloney* guidelines to the direct the jury and Ds were convicted of murder. On appeal the Court of Appeal quashed their conviction. This was upheld by House of Lords.

The *Moloney* guidelines were defective as they omitted the word 'probable'. Probability is important in deciding whether a consequence was intended.

Lord Scarman
'In my judgment, therefore, the *Moloney* guidelines as they stand are unsafe and misleading. They require a reference to

probability. They also require an explanation that the greater the probability of a consequence, the more likely it is that the consequence was foreseen and that if that consequence was foreseen the greater the probability is that that consequence was also intended'.

Nedrick [1986] 3 All ER 1, (1986) 83 Cr App R 267

D had a grudge against a woman. He poured paraffin through the letter box of her house and set it alight. A child died in the fire. D was convicted of murder but the Court of Appeal quashed the conviction and substituted one of manslaughter.

It was helpful for a jury to ask themselves two questions:

(1) How probable was the consequence which resulted from D's voluntary act? and
(2) Did D foresee that consequence?

The consequence had to be a virtual certainty and D must have realised that for there to be evidence on which to infer the D had the necessary intention.

Lord Lane CJ
'The jury should be directed that they are not entitled to infer the necessary intention unless they feel sure that death or serious bodily harm was a virtual certainty (barring some unforeseen intervention) as a result of the defendant's actions and that the defendant appreciated that such was the case'.

HL *Woollin* [1998] UKHL 28, [1999] 1 Cr App R 8

D lost his temper with his three-month-old son and threw him towards his pram. The child struck his head on a hard surface and died from a fractured skull.

The two questions in *Nedrick* were not helpful. The model direction from *Nedrick* should be used, but the word 'find' should be used rather than the word 'infer'.

The model direction should now be: 'the jury should be directed that they are not entitled to *find* the necessary intention unless they feel sure that death or serious bodily harm was a virtual certainty (barring some unforeseen intervention) as a result of the defendant's actions and that the defendant appreciated that such was the case'.

The word 'infer' is used in s 8 of the Criminal Justice Act 1967 and this is presumably why it was used in *Nedrick*. Does the substitution of the word 'find' improve the clarity of the direction to the jury? Also does the use of the word 'find' mean that foresight of consequence is intention and not merely evidence of it?

In the civil case of *Re A* (2000), doctors asked the courts whether they could operate to separate conjoined twins when they foresaw that this would kill the weaker twin. The Court of Appeal (Civil Division) clearly thought that *Woollin* laid down the rule that foresight of consequences **is** intention.

 Matthews and Alleyne [2003] EWCA Crim 192.

3.2 Recklessness

CA *Cunningham* [1957] 2 All ER 412, (1957) 41 Cr App R 155

D broke into a gas meter to steal money. In doing this, he fractured a gas pipe. Gas then leaked into the next door house where V was sleeping. D was charged under s 23 of the Offences against the Person Act 1861 with 'unlawfully and maliciously' administering a noxious substance to V endangering her life.

'Maliciously' in a statute has the meaning of either intention or subjective recklessness, ie D must have had intention OR realised there was a risk of the consequence occurring and gone on to take that risk.

Byrne J
'In any statutory definition of a crime, "malice" must be taken not in the old vague sense of wickedness in general, but as requiring either (1) an actual intention to do the particular kind of harm that in fact was done, or (2) recklessness as to whether such harm should occur or not (ie the accused has foreseen the risk that the particular kind of harm might be done, and yet has gone on to take the risk)'.

There need only be realisation of a risk for recklessness: whereas for specific intent D must realise that the consequence is a virtual certainty.

Metropolitan Police Commissioner v Caldwell
[1981] 1 All ER 961, (1981) 73 Cr App R 13

D had a grievance against the owner of a hotel. D got very drunk and decided to set fire to the hotel. He started a fire on the ground floor. This fire was put out quickly, without serious damage to the hotel. D was charged with arson under 1(2) of the Criminal Damage Act 1971. This requires that D intended or was reckless as to whether life was endangered. D claimed that he was so drunk he had not realised people's lives might be endangered. He was convicted.

It was held that 'reckless' covered two situations. The first is where D had realised the risk and the second where D had not thought about the possibility of any risk.

The second meaning of 'reckless' caused problems in cases where D was not capable of appreciating the risk involved in his conduct, even though a reasonable person would have realised there was a risk. This occurred in _Elliott v C_ [1983] 2 All ER 1005 where D was a 14-year-old girl with learning difficulties. Despite the fact that she did not appreciate the risk of her act, she was held to be guilty. This problem was eventually resolved when the House of Lords overruled _Caldwell_ in the case of _G and another_ (2003) (see next case).

 G and another [2003] UKHL 50

The defendants were two boys aged 11 and 12 years. During a night out camping, they went into the yard of a shop and set fire to some bundles of newspapers which they threw under a large wheelie bin. They then left the yard. They expected that as there was a concrete floor under the wheelie bin the fire would extinguish itself. In fact, the bin caught fire and this spread to the shop and other buildings, causing about £1 million worth of damage. The boys were convicted under both s 1 and s 3 of the Criminal Damage Act 1971. On appeal, the House of Lords quashed their conviction.

A defendant could not be guilty unless he had realised the risk and decided to take it. The House of Lords overruled the decision in *Caldwell*, holding that in that case the Law Lords had 'adopted an interpretation of section 1 of the 1971 Act which was beyond the range of feasible meanings'.

3.3 Gross negligence

CA *Bateman* (1925) 19 Cr App R 8

D was a doctor who attended a woman who was due to give birth. His supervision of her labour was negligent and she died.

The standard of negligence which has to be proved in manslaughter cases is considerably higher than the level which is sufficient for civil claims in negligence.

Lord Hewitt CJ
'In order to establish criminal liability, the facts must be such that, in the opinion of the jury, the negligence of the accused went beyond a mere matter of compensation between subjects

and showed such disregard for the life and safety of others as to amount to a crime against the state and conduct deserving of punishment'.

HL *Adomako* **[1994] 3 All ER 79, [1994] Crim LR 757**

D was an anaesthetist who failed to notice that during an operation a tube supplying oxygen to a patient had become disconnected. As a result, the patient died.

To establish gross negligent manslaughter, the elements of the civil tort of negligence must be present. These are:

- D must owe V a duty of care;
- D must be in breach of that duty;
- the breach must cause the death.

In addition, to impose criminal liability, the breach must be sufficiently serious to make it criminal behaviour.

Lord Mackay LC
'The ordinary principles of the law of negligence apply to ascertain whether or not the defendant has been in breach of a duty of care towards the victim who had died. If such a breach of duty is established the next question is whether that breach of duty caused the death of the victim. If so, the jury must go on to consider whether that breach of duty should be characterised as gross negligence and therefore a crime. This will depend on the seriousness of the breach of duty committed by the defendant in all the circumstances in which the defendant was placed when it occurred. The jury will have to consider whether the extent to

which the defendant's conduct departed from the proper standard of care incumbent upon him, involving as it must have done a risk of death to the patient, was such that it should be judged criminal'.

This places the decision as to whether the breach is criminal negligence on the jury. It has been argued that different juries may well apply different standards in making this decision. It can also be argued that the test is circular – the jury must decide that the breach is criminal and they do this by deciding that D's conduct should be judged as criminal.

3.4 Transferred malice

CR *Latimer* (1886) 17 QBD 359

D quarrelled with a man. During the quarrel, D aimed a blow with his belt at the man. The blow glanced off the man and struck and cut a woman on the face. D was found guilty under s 20 of the Offences Against the Person Act 1861.

An intention aimed at one person can be transferred to an unintended victim.

Coleridge CJ
'It is common knowledge that a man who has an unlawful and malicious intent against another, and, in attempting to carry it

out, injures a third person, is guilty of what the law deems malice against the person injured, because the offender is doing an unlawful act, and has that which the judges call general malice, and that is enough'.

 Pembliton (1874) LR 2 CCR 119

In the course of a fight with other men, D threw a stone at some of them. The stone missed the men, but struck and broke a window.

Where the type of crime is completely different to that intended, then there cannot be transferred malice.

 Attorney-General's Reference (No 3 of 1994) [1997] 3 All ER 936, [1998] 1 Cr App R 91

D stabbed his pregnant girlfriend. The girl recovered but the wound caused her baby to be born prematurely. As a result of the premature birth the child died at four months old. D was charged with the murder of the baby but the judge directed an acquittal, ruling that a foetus is not a person in law and so no conviction for either murder or manslaughter was possible in law.

The doctrine of transferred malice existed and was good law. However, in these circumstances it could not be used as a foetus was not a person. D could be guilty of unlawful act manslaughter. (See **Chapter 11**.)

CHAPTER 4

STRICT LIABILITY

ABSOLUTE LIABILITY
Larsonneur (1933)
An absolute offence can be committed through a state of affairs.
Not only need D have no *mens rea*, but D's act need not be voluntary.

COMMON LAW
Lemon and Whitehouse v Gay News (1979)
Blasphemy is a strict liability offence. It need not be proved that D intended to blaspheme

STRICT LIABILITY

STATUTORY OFFENCES
Sweet v Parsley (1969)
There is a presumption that *mens rea* is required
Gammon (Hong Kong) Ltd (1984)
The presumption that *mens rea* is required can only be displaced if it is clearly the effect of the statute
B (a minor) (2000)
The starting point is that *mens rea* is required
Sherras v de Rutzen (1895)
A genuine mistake can be a defence only if the offence is not one of strict liability

4.1 Absolute liability

 Larsonneur (1933) 24 Cr App R 74

D was an alien who had been ordered to leave the UK. She went to Eire, but the Irish police deported her and took her in police custody back to the UK where she was put in a cell. She was found guilty under the Aliens Order 1920 of 'being an alien to whom leave to land in the United Kingdom has been refused' was 'found in the United Kingdom'.

An absolute offence can be committed through a state of affairs. D's act in returning was not voluntary. She had no *mens rea*.

Should a state of affairs give rise to criminal liability? Not only did D not have any intention of returning to the UK, but her act was involuntary. She did not want to return to the UK, but was brought back by the Irish police. Is it just that there should be criminal liability in such a situation?

Winzar v Chief Constable of Kent, The Times, March 28, 1983; Co/1111/82 (Lexis) Queen's Bench Division.

4.2 Strict liability at common law

HL *Lemon and Whitehouse v Gay News*
[1979] 1 All ER 898, (1979) 68 Cr App R 381

A poem was published in *Gay News*, describing homosexual

acts done to the body of Christ after his crucifixion and also described his alleged homosexual practices during his lifetime. The editor and publishers were convicted of blasphemy.

The common law offence of blasphemy is a strict liability offence. It was not necessary to prove that the defendants intended to blaspheme.

4.3 Strict liability and statutory offences

HL *Sweet v Parsley* [1969] 1 All ER 347, (1969) 53 Cr App R 221

D rented a farmhouse out to students. The police found cannabis at the farmhouse and D was charged with 'being concerned in the management of premises used for the purpose of smoking cannabis resin'. D did not know that cannabis was being smoked there.

There was a presumption that the offence required *mens rea*. D was not guilty as she had no knowledge of the cannabis smoking.

Lord Reid
'[T]here has for centuries been a presumption that Parliament did not intend to make criminals of persons who were in no way blameworthy in what they did. That means that, whenever a section is silent as to *mens rea*, there is a presumption that, in order to give effect to the will of Parliament, we must read in words appropriate to require *mens rea*'.

Gammon (Hong Kong) Ltd v Attorney-General of Hong Kong
[1984] 2 All ER 503, (1984) 80 Cr App R 194

The appellants were charged with deviating from building
work in a material way from the approved plan, contrary to
the Hong Kong Building Ordinances. It had to be decided
whether it was necessary to prove that they knew that their
deviation was material. It was held that it was not necessary: it
was a strict liability offence and they were found guilty.

The presumption in favour of *mens rea* being required before
D can be convicted applies to statutory offences and can be
displaced only if this is clearly or by necessary implication the
effect of the statute.

HL **B (a minor) v DPP** [2000] 1 All ER 833, [2000] 2 Cr App R 65

 D, a 15-year-old boy, asked a 13-year-old girl on a
bus to give him a 'shiner', (ie have oral sex with
him). He believed she was over the age of 14. He
was charged with inciting a child under the age of
14 to commit an act of gross indecency under s
1(1) of the Indecency with Children Act 1960.

 The starting point for the courts was the
presumption that *mens rea* was intended. The
judgment in *Sweet v Parsley* (1969) was approved.

 The case identified the major elements which have
to be considered in deciding whether the offence is
one of strict liability as:

• the presumption of *mens rea*;
• the lack of words of intention;

- whether that presumption was negatived by necessary implication;
- the severity of the punishment;
- the purpose of the section;
- evidential problems;
- effectiveness of strict liability.

Sherras v de Rutzen [1895] 1 QB 918

D was convicted of supplying liquor to a constable on duty, under s 16(2) of the Licensing Act 1872. Normally, local police who were on duty wore an armband on their uniform. An on-duty police officer removed his armband before entering D's public house. He was served by D's daughter in the presence of D. Neither D nor his daughter made any enquiry as to whether the policeman was on duty. D thought that the constable was off duty because he was not wearing his armband. D appealed.

Held that the offence was not one of strict liability and therefore a genuine mistake provided the defendant with a defence.

CHAPTER 5

PARTICIPATION

ACTUS REUS
Attorney-General's Reference (No 1 of 1975) (1975)
Aid, abet, counsel and procure have different meanings
Giannetto (1997)
Abetting can be 'mere encouragement upwards'
Wilcox v Jeffery (1951)
Presence at a public performance can be sufficient
Clarkson and others (1971)
Mere presence at the scene of a crime is not enough
Calhaem (1985)
There is no need for a causal link between counseling and the offence

MENS REA
National Coal Board v Gamble (1958)
Intention to do the act which aids and abets, but there can be indifference to the offence
Bainbridge (1959)
There is no need to know the details of the offence the principal will commit
DPP for Northern Ireland v Maxwell (1978)
It is enough for D to know that it is one of a number of possible crimes
Attorney-General's Reference (No 1 of 1975) 1975
For procuring there is no need to prove a shared intention

SECONDARY PARTICIPATION

JOINT ENTERPRISE
Powell: English (1997)
There need only be foresight or contemplation that the principal might commit the offence
Stewart and Schofield (1995)
If a secondary party does not foresee or contemplate serious injury or death, they cannot be liable for murder
Uddin (1998)
If all intend serious injury or death, they are all liable for murder
If a very different weapon is used, D is not liable for the death

WITHDRAWAL FROM A JOINT ENTERPRISE
Becerra and Cooper (1975)
D must effectively communicate his withdrawal
Mitchell and King (1999)
Where there is spontaneous violence then walking away is sufficient for withdrawal

5.1 *Actus reus* of secondary participation

CA *Attorney-General's Reference* **(No 1 of 1975)**
[1975] 2 All ER 684, (1975) 61 Cr App R 118

D, who knew that a friend was going to drive home, laced his non-alcoholic drink with alcohol. When the friend was charged with driving while over the limit for alcohol (s 6(1) Road Traffic Act 1972), D was charged with aiding, abetting, counselling and procuring that offence. The trial judge ruled that there was no case to answer as there was no meeting of minds.

(1) Each of the words 'aid', 'abet', 'counsel' and 'procure' has a different meaning.
(2) To 'procure' means to produce by endeavour.
(3) There must be a causal link between the procuring and the commission of the offence.

Lord Widgery CJ
'(1) We approach s 8 of the [Accessories and Abettors] Act of 1861 on the basis that the words should be given their ordinary meaning, if possible. We approach the section on the basis also that if four words are employed here, 'aid, abet, counsel or procure,' the probability is that there is a difference between each of those four words and the other three, because if there were no such difference, then Parliament would be wasting time in using four words when two or three would do.

(2) To procure means to produce by endeavour. You procure a thing by setting out to see that it happens and taking the appropriate steps to produce that happening.

(3) Causation here is important. You cannot procure an offence unless there is a causal link between what you do and the commission of the offence'.

Later cases do not show a need to set out to produce a result by endeavour. The causal link is the important factor. In *Millward* [1994] Crim LR 527 a farmer gave instructions for a poorly maintained tractor and trailer to be driven on a public road. The trailer became detached, hit a car and killed the driver. D was convicted of procuring the offence of causing death by reckless driving, even though he certainly did not set out to produce that result through endeavour. *Millward* also illustrates that a secondary party may be guilty, even though the principal is acquitted.

CA *Giannetto* [1997] 1 Cr App R 1

D was convicted of the murder of his wife. The prosecution relied on the fact that the wife had been murdered either by D himself or by a hired killer on D's behalf. D appealed on the basis that, as the prosecution could not prove whether he or another person had killed the wife, he should have been acquitted. The Court of Appeal held that as he had the intention to murder and the act had been carried out, it did not matter whether he was the principal or a secondary party.

For abetting, any involvement from 'mere encouragement upwards' is sufficient. Encouragement can be as little as patting on the back, nodding, or saying 'Oh goody' when told of the principal's intention to commit a particular crime.

Wilcox v Jeffery [1951] 1 All ER 464

Wilcox knew that an American saxophonist was not allowed to enter the United Kingdom. Despite this, Wilcox met him at the airport and attended a concert at which the American played. D was convicted of aiding and abetting the contravention of the Aliens Order 1920.

Where presence at a public performance encourages that performance, then the presence is sufficient for aiding and abetting.

 Clarkson and others [1971] 3 All ER 344, (1971) 55 Cr App R 445

D and another soldier entered a room within army barracks where a woman was being raped. They remained in the room while the rape continued but did nothing.

Being present but doing nothing is not sufficient to make D a secondary party. Non-interference to prevent a crime is not itself a crime.

 Calhaem [1985] 2 All ER 266, (1985) 81 Cr App R 131

D was infatuated with her solicitor. She hired a 'hitman' to kill a woman with whom the solicitor had been having an affair. The hitman claimed that he had decided not to go through with the plan to kill the woman, but when he saw her he went berserk and killed her. D argued that the causal

connection between her acts and the killing was broken when the hitman decided of his own accord to kill V.

There is no need for any causal connection between the counselling and the offence.

Parker LJ
'We must therefore approach the question raised on the basis that we should give to the word "counsel" its ordinary meaning, which is, as the judge said, "advise", "solicit" or something of that sort. There is no implication in the word itself that there should be any causal connection between the counselling and the offence'.

5.2 *Mens rea* of secondary participation

QBD | *National Coal Board v Gamble*
[1958] 3 All ER 203, (1958) 42 Cr App R 240

A weighbridge operator employed by the National Coal Board issued a ticket to a lorry driver, although the operator knew that the lorry was overloaded. The Board was convicted as a secondary party to the offence of using a motor lorry on a road with a load weighing more than that permitted.

The *mens rea* for secondary participation is the intention to do the act which aids or abets. D can be guilty as a secondary party even if he does not care whether the offence is committed or not.

Bainbridge [1959] 3 All ER 200, (1959) 43 Cr App R 194

D bought oxygen cutting equipment on behalf of others. He knew that the others were going to use the equipment for criminal purposes, though he did not know the exact details.

A secondary party can be guilty where he knows the type of offence that the principal is going to commit. It does not matter that he does not know the details.

DPP for Northern Ireland v Maxwell [1978] 3 All ER 1140, (1979) 68 Cr App R 128

D guided terrorists in Northern Ireland to a pub. He knew that some sort of attack was to be carried out there, but he did not know exactly what.

Bainbridge was correctly decided. It was not necessary to prove that D knew that exact offence, or even the exact type of offence.

Lord Scarman
'[In *Bainbridge* the Court of Appeal] refused to limit criminal responsibility by reference to knowledge by the accused of the type or class of crime intended by those whom he assisted … The guilt of an accessory springs from the fact that he contemplates the commission of one (or more) of a number of crimes by the principal and he intentionally lends his assistance in order that such a crime will be committed'.

CA *Attorney-General's Reference* (No 1 of 1975)
[1975] 2 All ER 684, (1975) 61 Cr App R 118

See **5.1**.

Where the prosecution relies on the secondary party procuring the offence, there is no need to prove a shared intention.

5.3 Joint enterprise

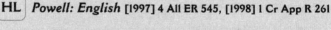

HL *Powell: English* [1997] 4 All ER 545, [1998] 1 Cr App R 261

These two cases were heard in a joined appeal (*Powell*)
D and two other men went to buy drugs at the house of a drug dealer. When the dealer opened the door, one of the other men shot him.

(*English*)
D took part with another man in a joint enterprise to attack and injure a police officer with wooden posts. During the attack the other man stabbed and killed the officer. English did not know that the other man was carrying a knife.

Foresight or contemplation that the principal may commit the offence is sufficient for the *mens rea* of an accomplice.

This decision means that in order to be convicted, a lower level of intention is sufficient for a secondary party to be convicted of murder than for a principal. This was acknowledged by the House of Lords when Lord Steyn said: 'Recklessness may suffice in the case of the secondary party but it does not in the case of the primary offender. The answer to this supposed anomaly is to be found in practical and policy considerations.'

This causes particular problems in murder cases as the judge has no discretion in sentencing. Is it just that a secondary party, who did not personally carry out the killing, can be convicted on a lower level of intention and so face a mandatory life sentence?

 Chan Wing-Siu v R [1984] 3 All ER 877, (1984) 80 Cr App R 117.

 ### Stewart and Schofield
[1995] 3 All ER 159, [1995] 1 Cr App R 441

Ds set out with another man, L, to rob a shop. They knew that L had with him a scaffolding bar and that it might be used to cause some injury. In fact L beat the shopkeeper to death. L was convicted of murder; Ds were convicted of unlawful act manslaughter.

As the secondary parties had not foreseen V would be seriously hurt or killed, they were not guilty of murder.

Uddin [1998] 2 All ER 744, [1999] 1 Cr App R 319

D was one of six men who attacked V with poles and bars. In the course of the attack, V was stabbed by one of the men and died from the stab wound. D was convicted of murder and appealed on the basis that the judge had failed to direct the jury that D could only be guilty of murder if he foresaw the possibility that a knife would be used.

The Court of Appeal set out a series of principles on liability as a secondary participant. The main ones are:

(1) Where several persons join in a fatal attack on V, intending to inflict serious harm, they are jointly liable for murder. However, if the fatal injury is caused solely by the actions of one person of a type entirely different from actions which the others foresaw, only that person is guilty of murder.

(2) In deciding whether the actions are of 'a type entirely different' the use of a weapon is a significant factor. If its character (eg its propensity to cause death) is different from any weapon used or contemplated by the others, then they are not responsible for the death unless it is proved that they knew or foresaw the likelihood of the use of such a weapon.

(3) If some or all of the others are using weapons which could be regarded as equally likely to inflict fatal injuries, the mere fact that a different weapon was used is immaterial.

5.4 Withdrawal from a joint enterprise

Becerra and Cooper (1975) 62 Cr App R 212

B and C broke into a house in order to steal. B gave C a knife to use if anyone interrupted them. When they were interrupted by V, B said 'There's a bloke coming. Let's go' and jumped out of a window. C stabbed and killed V. Both B and C were convicted of murder.

To withdraw from a joint enterprise effectively, B must communicate his withdrawal. Merely saying 'Let's go' was not sufficient for communicating withdrawal where B had already given C the knife.

Rook [1993] 2 All ER 955, (1993) 97 Cr App R 327.

Mitchell and King [1999] Crim LR 496

An unplanned fight broke out in a restaurant and continued in to the street. D1 and D2 were involved in the fight during which V was badly beaten. D1 then dropped a stick, stopped fighting and walked away. D2 picked up the stick and renewed the attack on V who later died.

Where spontaneous violence occurs, D can withdraw without communicating his withdrawal to others involved in the attack.

CHAPTER 6

INCHOATE OFFENCES

ATTEMPTS
A-G's reference (No 1 of 1992) (1993)
Need not have performed the last act before the crime proper, nor reached the point of no return
Gullefer (1987)
Must have gone beyond purely preparatory acts and be 'embarked on the crime proper'
Millard and Vernon (1987)
Recklessness as to a consequence is not sufficient *mens rea* for an attempt
Shivpuri (1987)
Even when the complete offence is impossible to commit, there can be an attempt

INCITEMENT
Invicta Plastics Ltd v Clare (1976)
Incitement can be implied
Incitement can be encouragement or threats
DPP v Armstrong (2000)
No need for the person incited to intend to commit offence
Fitzmaurice (1983)
There can not be incitement of an impossible offence

INCHOATE OFFENCES

STATUTORY CONSPIRACY
Reed (1982)
There is a statutory conspiracy when an offence will 'necessarily' be committed if the plan is carried out as intended
Jackson (1985)
A plan for a contingency which necessarily involved the commission of an offence is sufficient
Yip Chiu-Cheung v R (1994)
D and at least one other must intend that the offence be committed

CONSPIRACY TO DEFRAUD
Scott v MPC (1975)
(1) Not necessary to prove that economic loss was suffered, but V's economic interests must be put at risk.
(2) Deception is not a required element of the offence
Wai Yu-tsang (1991)
It is enough if anyone may be prejudiced in any way by the fraud

6.1 Incitement

Invicta Plastics Ltd v Clare [1976] Crim LR 131

D advertised a device which warned drivers when they were approaching a police radar sped trap. The company was prosecuted for inciting motorists to receive radio transmissions without a licence, contrary to s 1(1) of the Wireless Telegraphy Act 1949.

(1) Incitement is normally encouragement or persuasion but can also be by threats or pressure.
(2) The *actus reus* of incitement may be implied rather than express.
(3) Incitement is determined by looking at D's acts as a whole.

Park J cited with approval Lord Denning's statement on the meaning of incitement in *Race Relations Board v Applin* [1973] QB 815:

'[It is] suggested that to "incite" means to urge or spur on by advice, encouragement, and persuasion, and not otherwise. I do not think the word is so limited, at any rate in the context. A person may "incite" another to do an act by threatening or by pressure, as well as by persuasion'.

DPP v Armstrong [2000] Crim LR 379

D phoned J to ask for pornography of girls 'not younger than say 12 years'. J was in fact an undercover police officer investigating paedophilia. D was charged with inciting J to commit the offence of distributing indecent photographs of children. The magistrates dismissed the case on the basis that the person incited must have 'parity of *mens rea*' with the inciter. The Divisional Court allowed the prosecution's appeal.

There is no need for the person incited to intend to commit the offence. The offence of incitement is accurately set out in cl 47 of the draft Criminal Code:

'A person is guilty of incitement to commit an offence or offences if –

(a) he incites another to do or cause to be done acts which, if done, will involve the commission of the offence or offences by the other; and

(b) he intends or believes that the other, if he acts as incited, shall or will do so with the fault required for the offence or offences'.

CA *Fitzmaurice* [1983] 1 All ER 189, (1983) 76 Cr App R 17

D's father asked D to find someone to take part in robbing a woman who was taking wages to a bank. In fact the robbery was a fiction put forward by D's father so that he could claim reward money. D, believing that the robbery was going to take place, recruited B to take part in the supposed robbery.

If the offence incited is impossible to commit then the inciter will not be guilty. However, in this case D was guilty as it would have been possible for B to rob a woman at the place named.

6.2 Conspiracy

CA *Reed* [1982] Crim LR 819

D and another man agreed that the other man should visit individuals who were contemplating suicide and, depending on his assessment of the situation, either discourage them or actively help them to commit suicide. They were charged with conspiracy to murder.

Provided an offence will 'necessarily' be committed if the plan is carried out as intended, D will be guilty of statutory conspiracy.

Donaldson LJ

'(1) A and B agree to drive from London to Edinburgh in a time which can be achieved without exceeding the speed limit but only if the traffic is exceptionally light. Their agreement will not necessarily involve the commission of any offence.

(2) A and B agree to rob a bank if, when they arrive at the bank, it is safe to do so. Their agreement will necessarily involve the commission of the offence of robbery if it is carried out in accordance with their intentions'.

CA *Jackson* [1985] Crim LR 442

Three men agreed to shoot another in the leg if he was convicted, so that there would be mitigating circumstances when he was sentenced. They were convicted of conspiring to pervert the course of justice.

Where the plan was for a contingency taking place, then provided that plan necessarily involved the commission of an offence D was guilt of conspiracy.

Anderson [1986] AC 27, (1985) 81 Cr App R 253.

PC *Yip Chiu-Cheung v R* [1994] 2 All ER 924, (1994) 99 Cr App R 406

D conspired with N to traffic in heroin. N was in fact an undercover drugs enforcement agent. D appealed against his conviction on the basis that N did not intend to carry out the offence and so could not be a conspirator.

D and at least one other must intend that the offence be committed. In this case N was intending to take the drugs into Australia and so had the intention to commit the offence, although he knew he would not be prosecuted.

HL *Scott v Metropolitan Police Commissioner* [1975] AC 818, (1974) 60 Cr App R 124

D agreed with employees in cinemas that they would temporarily remove films so that D could make pirate copies. The cinema owners were unaware of the plan so there was no deception, nor did the owners suffer economic loss.

(1) It is not necessary to prove that economic loss was suffered. It is enough that V's economic interests are put at risk.
(2) Deception is not a required element of the offence.

PC

Wai Yu-tsang v R [1991] 4 All ER 664, (1994) 94 Cr App R 264

D and employees of a bank agreed to conceal the fact that cheques which the bank had purchased had been dishonoured. D had done this in order to prevent a 'run' on the bank.

Conspiracy to defraud is not limited to economic loss, nor to the idea of depriving someone of something of value. It is enough if anyone may be prejudiced in any way by the fraud.

6.3 Attempts

CA

Attorney-General's Reference (No 1 of 1992)
[1993] 2 All ER 190, (1993) 96 Cr App R 298

D dragged a girl up some steps to a shed. He lowered his trousers and interfered with her private parts. His penis remained flaccid. He argued that he could not therefore attempt to commit rape.

D need not have performed the last act before the crime proper, nor need he have reached the point of no return.

Gullefer [1987] Crim LR 195, [1990] 3 All ER 882

D jumped onto a race track in order to have the race declared void and so enable him to reclaim money he had bet on it. His conviction for attempting to steal was quashed because his action was merely preparatory to committing the offence.

'More than merely preparatory' means that the defendant must have gone beyond purely preparatory acts and be 'embarked on the crime proper'.

* *Geddes* [1996] Crim LR 894;
* *Campbell* (1990) 93 Cr App R 350.

 Boyle and Boyle [1987] Crim LR 574

The defendants were found standing by a door of which the lock and one hinge were broken. Their conviction for attempted burglary was upheld.

Embarking on the crime proper is the test. In this case once Ds had entered they would be committing burglary, so trying to gain entry was an attempt.

Jones [1990] 3 All ER 886, (1990) 91 Cr App R 351.

CA *Easom* **[1971] 2 All ER 945, (1971) 55 Cr App R 410**

D picked up a woman's handbag in a cinema, rummaged through it, then put it back on the floor without removing anything from it. His conviction for theft of the bag and its contents was quashed. The Court of Appeal also refused to substitute a conviction for attempted theft of the bag and named contents (including a purse and a pen) as there was no evidence that D intended to steal the items.

To prove attempted theft, the *mens rea* for theft must be proved.

Where there is a conditional intent, ie D intended stealing if there was anything worth stealing, D could be charged with an attempt to steal some or all of the contents.

 CA *Millard and Vernon* **[1987] Crim LR 393**

Ds repeatedly pushed against a wooden fence on a stand at a football ground. The prosecution alleged that they were trying to break it and they were convicted of attempted criminal damage. The Court of Appeal quashed their convictions.

Recklessness as to a consequence is not sufficient *mens rea* for an attempt. This is so even where recklessness would suffice for the completed offence.

Shivpuri [1987] AC 1, (1986) 83 Cr App R 178

D thought he was dealing in prohibited drugs. In fact, it was snuff and harmless vegetable matter. He was convicted of attempting to be knowingly concerned in dealing with prohibited drugs.

Subsections 1(2) and 1(3) of the Criminal Attempts Act 1981 meant that a person could be guilty of an attempt even if the commission of the full offence was impossible.

The decision in *Shivpuri* overruled the case of *Anderton v Ryan* [1985] 2 All ER 335, (1985) 81 Cr App R 166 which had been decided a year earlier. The House of Lords accepted that its decision in *Anderton v Ryan* had been wrong and used the Practice Statement to overrule it.

CHAPTER 7

CAPACITY

MENTALLY ILL
Unfitness to plead
Antoine (2000)
Following a finding of
unfitness to plead a jury
should be empanelled to
decide if D did the act
alleged
Insanity: see **8.1**
Diminished
responsibility: see **11.2**

CORPORATIONS
P&O European Ferries
(Dover) Ltd (1991)
A corporation can be liable for
manslaughter
Bolton (Engineering) v TJ
Graham (1956)
There are people who
represent the mind and
will of the company
Tesco Supermarket v
Natrass (1972)
Only those at a sufficiently high
managerial level can make
the company liable

CAPACITY

VICARIOUS LIABILITY
Coppen v Moore (1898)
An act done within the scope of employment
can make the employer liable
Adams v Camfoni (1929)
An act outside of the scope of employment does
not make the employer liable
Allen v Whitehead (1930)
Where there is full delegation the
knowledge of the delegate will be imputed
to the delegator
Vane v Yiannopoullos (1964)
Where there is only partial delegation the
knowledge of the delegate will NOT be
imputed to the delegator

7.1 Unfitness to plead

 Antoine **[2000] 2 All ER 208, [2000] 2 Cr App R 94**

D was charged with murder but was found by a jury to be unfit to plead. A new jury then tried D to decide if he had committed the act of murder. He wanted that jury to consider whether he was suffering from diminished responsibility.

Section 4A of the Criminal Procedure (Insanity and Unfitness to Plead) Act 1991 means that the jury in the second hearing are only concerned with the *actus reus* and not the mental element of the offence.

Lord Hutton
'The purpose of s 4A is to strike a fair balance between the need to protect a defendant who has, in fact, done nothing wrong and is unfit to plead at his trial and the need to protect the public from a defendant who has committed an injurious act which would constitute a crime if done with the requisite *mens rea*'.

See the defence of insanity at **8.1** and the defence of diminished responsibility at **11.2**.

7.2 Corporations

 P&O European Ferries (Dover) Ltd (1991) 93 Cr App R 72

The cross-channel ferry, the *Herald of Free Enterprise*, sailed
out of Zeebrugge harbour with her bow doors open. This
caused the ferry to capsize, killing 192 people. The operating
company, P & O, and seven individuals were charged with
manslaughter.

A corporation can be liable for manslaughter, but only where a
person sufficiently senior in management could be proved
to have had the necessary guilty mind so as to make the
company guilty.

HL Bolton (Engineering) Co Ltd v TJ Graham & Sons Ltd
[1956] 3 All ER 624

The case involved civil proceedings about a tenancy. The
landlord was a limited company and the question arose
whether the directors' intentions could be imputed to the
company.

Where senior officials of a company have intention, that
intention can be imputed to the company.

Lord Denning
'A company may in many ways be likened to a human body.
It has a brain and a nerve centre which controls what it does.
It also has hands which hold the tools and act in accordance
with directions from the centre. Some of the people in the
company are mere servants and agents who are nothing more
than hands to do the work and cannot be said to represent the
mind or will. Others are directors and managers who represent

the directing mind and will of the company and control what it does. The state of mind of these managers is the state of mind of the company and is treated by the law as such'.

 Tesco Supermarkets Ltd v Natrass [1972] AC 153

A Tesco store advertised packets of washing machine powder at a reduced price. An employee did not tell the store manager when all the reduced price packets were sold and the adverts continued. The company was charged under s 11 of the Trade Descriptions Act 1968 with giving a false indication as to price.

A store manager was at too low a level of management to be the 'mind and the will' of a company for the purpose of making the company criminally liable.

 Attorney-General's Reference (No 2 of 1999) [2000] 3 All ER 187

A high-speed passenger train collided with a freight train, killing seven people. The driver had failed to see a series of warning lights and two safety devices in the cab were switched off.

A company could not be convicted of gross negligence manslaughter where there was no evidence establishing guilt of an identified human individual for the same crime.

See gross negligence manslaughter at **11.5**.

7.3 Vicarious liability

DC · *Coppen v Moore (No 2)* [1898] 2 QB 306

The appellant owned six shops. He had issued instructions that any hams sold in them must not be given a specific place of origin. Despite this, an assistant in one of the shops sold a ham (which was American) as 'a Scotch ham'. The appellant was convicted of selling goods to which a false trade description had been applied.

Where an offence is committed by an act such as 'selling', 'using' or 'driving' then a corporation can be liable for acts of its employees, provided that such act is done by an employee acting within the scope of employment.

Lord Russell CJ
'[I]t was clearly the intention of the legislature to make the master criminally liable for acts [which were done within the scope or in the course of employment]'.

DC · *Adams v Camfoni* [1929] 1 KB 95

D, a licensee, was charged with selling alcohol outside the hours permitted by his licence. In fact, the sale had been made by a messenger boy who had no authority to sell anything. D's conviction was quashed.

An employer is not liable for the acts of his employees where the act done was outside the scope of the employment.

DC *Allen v Whitehead* [1930] 1 KB 211

D was the owner and licensee of a café. He employed a manager to run the café. He instructed the manager not to allow prostitutes to enter the café. The manager allowed women, whom he knew to be prostitutes, to use the premises.

The knowledge or intention of the person to whom responsibility has been delegated is treated as being the knowledge or intention of the principal.

HL *Vane v Yiannopoullos* [1964] 3 All ER 820

D was the licensee of a restaurant. He had given instruction to a waitress not to serve alcohol to people unless they ordered a meal. The restaurant was on two floors and, while the licensee was on another floor, the waitress served alcohol to two people who did not order a meal. D was charged with 'knowingly selling intoxicating liquor to persons to whom he was not entitled to sell'. His conviction was quashed.

There must be complete delegation to make the principal liable through the knowledge or intention of his servant.

CHAPTER 8

INSANITY, AUTOMATISM AND INTOXICATION

INSANITY

M'Naghten's case (1843)
Presumed sane until the contrary is proved. Must have a defect of reason caused by disease of the mind so as not to know the nature and quality of act or that what he was doing was wrong

Sullivan (1984)
Impairment can be organic or functional and need not be permanent

Burgess (1991)
A mental disorder which manifests itself in violence and is prone to recur is a disease of the mind

Hennessy (1989)
An internal cause is a disease of the mind, even where the disease is a physical one such as diabetes

Windle (1952)
If D knows he is doing wrong, the defence of insanity is not available to him

INSANITY, AUTOMATISM INTOXICATION

AUTOMATISM

Bratty v A-G for NI (1961)
Automatism is an act done by the muscles without any control by the mind

Hill v Baxter (1958)
For the defence of automatism the cause must an external one

A-G's Ref (No 2 of 1992) (1993)
Reduced or partial awareness is insufficient for the defence

Bailey (1983)
(1) Self-induced automatism is a defence to a specific intent offence
(2) Reckless self-induced automatism is NOT a defence to a basic intent offence

Hardie (1984)
If D is not reckless in getting into an automatic state then automatism is a defence to a basic intent offence

INTOXICATION

A-G for NI v Gallagher (1963)
A drunken intent is sufficient for *mens rea*

DPP v Majewski (1976)
Voluntary intoxication is not available as a defence, for a basic intent offence

Kingston (1994)
The defence of involuntary intoxication is not available if D has the *mens rea* for the offence

8.1 Insanity

M'Naghten's Case (1843) 10 Cl & F 200

D was charged with the murder of the Prime Minister's secretary. He was found not guilty by reason of insanity. Following this case, the issue of insanity was debated in the House of Lords and the judges were asked to explain the law.

(1) Every man is presumed to be sane and to possess a sufficient degree of reason to be responsible for his crimes.
(2) To prove the defence of insanity, a defendant must show that he was labouring under such a defect of reason, from disease of the mind, as not to know the nature and quality of the act he was doing, or if he did know it, that he did not know he was doing what was wrong.

HL | ***Sullivan***
[1984] AC 156, (1983) 77 Cr App R 176

While D was at the home of a friend, he had an epileptic fit. In the course of that fit he attacked and injured the friend. D argued that he should be allowed the defence of automatism. The trial judge ruled that his defence was insanity.

Where D is suffering from a disease of the mind, then this can be within the definition of insanity.

The disease can be one which causes a transient or intermittent impairment of reason, memory or understanding. The condition need not be permanent.

Bratty v Attorney-General for Northern Ireland
[1961] 3 All ER 523, (1961) 46 Cr App R 1

D strangled a girl. He gave evidence that 'a blackness' came over him and he did not realise what he had done. There was evidence that he might have been suffering from epilepsy. His defence of insanity was rejected and he was convicted of murder.

If an involuntary act was due to a disease of the mind then the defence is insanity. If the involuntariness of the act was caused by an external factor, then, provided there is evidence to raise the issue, the jury must consider the defence of automatism.

Lord Denning
'Automatism is an act done by the muscles without any control by the mind, such as a spasm, a reflex action or a convulsion; or an act done by a person who is not conscious of what he is doing such as an act done whilst suffering from concussion or whilst sleep-walking'.

Burgess [1991] 2 All ER 769, (1991) 93 Cr App R 41

D attacked a girl, with whom he had been watching a video, with a bottle and the video recorder and then put his hands round her neck. He claimed he was sleepwalking and that this should give him the defence of automatism. It was ruled that the evidence was of an internal cause and so the correct defence was insanity.

Any mental disorder which has manifested itself in violence
and which is prone to recur is a disease of the mind. Thus the
correct defence is insanity.

 CA *Hennessy* [1989] 2 All ER 9, (1989) 89 Cr App R 10

D was a diabetic who needed insulin to control the condition.
He was charged with taking a car and driving whilst
disqualified. His defence was that because he had failed to take
his insulin, this had caused him to suffer hyperglycaemia. The
trial judge ruled that this was an internal factor and therefore
the defence of insanity.

Where the cause of the involuntary behaviour is an internal
cause, then it is a disease of the mind and the correct defence
is insanity.

The decisions in this case and *Burgess* (1991) (above) have
extended the meaning of insanity in the criminal law far
beyond any medical definition. It is invidious that those with a
physical disease such as diabetes should come within the
definition of insanity.

Kemp [1956] 1 All ER 249, (1956) 40 Cr App R 121.

Quick [1973] 3 All ER 347, (1973) 57 Cr App R 722

D, a nurse, was convicted of causing actual bodily harm to a patient. He said he had failed to eat after taking insulin for his diabetes. This had caused hypoglycaemia. The trial judge ruled this was the defence of insanity. The conviction was quashed because it was an external cause (the drug insulin) which had led to the involuntary act.

Where there is an external cause, then it is not a disease of the mind, and the correct defence is automatism.

The decisions in *Hennessy* and *Quick* have created an anomaly. If the cause is the failure to take insulin, this is an internal factor and considered a disease of the mind within the rules of insanity. However, if the cause is the taking of insulin, then this is an external cause and not within the rules of insanity.

 Windle [1952] 2 QB 826, (1952) 36 Cr App R 85

D killed his wife by giving her about 100 tablets of aspirin. There was evidence that he was suffering from a mental illness. However, because he told the police 'I suppose they will hang me for this' he was aware that what he had done was wrong.

Where D knows that what he is doing is wrong then he cannot bring himself within the *M'Naghten* Rules. The defence of insanity is not available to him.

This case emphasises that those with mental illness may be denied the defence of insanity, even though they are not fully responsible for their actions. To meet this criticism the defence of diminished responsibility was created in 1957 to provide a partial defence to murder.

8.2 Automatism

DC *Hill v Baxter* [1958] 1 All ER 193, (1958) 42 Cr App R 51

D was acquitted of dangerous driving by magistrates who accepted that he remembered nothing for some distance before going through a halt sign. The Divisional Court allowed the prosecution's appeal and remitted the case back to the magistrates with a direction to convict as there was no evidence to support a defence of automatism.

Where an external cause makes D's actions involuntary, the defence of automatism is available.

The court approved the judgment of Humphrey J in *Kay v Butterworth* (where he said):

'A person should not be made liable at the criminal law who, through no fault of his own, becomes unconscious when driving, as, for example, a person who has been struck by a stone or overcome by a sudden illness, or when the car has been put temporarily out of his control owing to his being attacked by a swarm of bees'.

T [1990] Crim LR 256

D was raped. Three days later she took part in a robbery and an assault. She claimed that at the time she was suffering from post traumatic stress disorder as a result of the rape and that she had acted in a dream-like state. The trial judge allowed the defence of automatism to go to the jury, but D was convicted.

An external cause of an automatic state is the defence of non-insane automatism rather than insanity.

This decision is only at Crown Court level. The recent trend of the appeal courts has been to regard behaviour which occurs after an external shock as having its source in the internal psychological or emotional state of D so that it provides a defence of insanity rather than non-insane automatism.

Rabey (1980) SCR 513 Canada

Attorney-General's Reference (No 2 of 1992)
[1993] 4 All ER 683, (1993) 99 Cr App R 429

D was a lorry driver who, after driving for several hours, drove along the hard shoulder of a motorway for about half a mile and hit a broken-down car.

Reduced or partial awareness is not enough to found a defence of automatism.

CA — *Bailey* [1983] 2 All ER 503, (1983) 77 Cr App Rep 76

D was a diabetic who failed to eat properly after taking insulin. This caused a hypoglycaemic state during which he hit V on the head with an iron bar. The trial judge ruled that the defence of automatism was not available. It was held that this ruling was wrong although D's conviction stood as there was insufficient evidence to raise the defence of automatism.

(1) Automatism, even if self-induced, is a defence to an offence which requires the prosecution to prove specific intent.

(2) Self-induced automatism is also a defence to a basic intent offence if D was not reckless in getting into that state.

(3) Where D is reckless in getting into a self-induced state of automatism, then he cannot rely on the defence for a basic intent offence.

CA — *Hardie* [1984] 3 All ER 848, (1984) 80 Cr App R 157

D, who was upset by the breakdown of a relationship, took some Valium belonging to his ex-girlfriend. She encouraged him to do this stating that it would calm him down. He later started a fire in the bedroom of their flat. He was charged under s 1(2) of the Criminal Damage Act 1971. D argued that the effect of the drug prevented him having the *mens rea* for the offence. The trial judge ruled against this. The Court of Appeal quashed the conviction.

To be guilty of a basic intent offence, D must have acted recklessly in taking the drug which caused the automatic state. Where the intoxicating effect of a drug is not generally known then the prosecution need to prove that D knew there was a risk it could make him intoxicated.

8.3 Intoxication

HL *Attorney-General for Northern Ireland v Gallagher*
[1963] AC 349, (1961) 45 Cr App Rep 316

D decided to kill his wife. He then bought a knife and a bottle of whisky. After drinking a large amount of the whisky he killed his wife. He claimed that at the time of the killing he was drunk. He was convicted of murder but the conviction was quashed by the Court of Appeal. The House of Lords restored his conviction.

Where D forms the required *mens rea* for an offence then drunkenness is not a defence. This is the law both for specific intent offences and basic intent offences.

Lord Denning
'If a man, whilst sane and sober, forms an intention to kill and makes preparation for it, knowing it is a wrong thing to do, and then gets himself drunk so as to give himself Dutch courage to do the killing, and while drunk carries out his intention, he cannot rely on this self-induced drunkenness as a defence to a charge of murder'.

HL *DPP v Majweski*
[1976] 2 All ER 142, (1976) 62 Cr App R 262

As a result of taking drugs and alcohol, D became aggressive and assaulted a barman and police officers who were called to the scene. He claimed he had 'completely blanked out' and did not know what he was doing. He was convicted of offences of assault occasioning actual bodily harm and of assaulting a police officer in the execution of his duty.

Where an offence is one of basic intent then voluntary intoxication is not available as a defence.

Lord Elwyn-Jones LC
'If a man, of his own volition, takes a substance which causes him to cast off the restraints of reason and conscience, no wrong is done to him by holding him answerably criminally for any injury he may do while in that condition. His course of conduct in reducing himself by drugs and drink to that condition in my view supplies the evidence of *mens rea*, of guilty mind certainly sufficient for crimes of basic intent'.

In such situations the recklessness is at the point when D consumes enough alcohol to make him drunk. The *actus reus* may be several hours later when D actually commits an assault. Is there coincidence of *mens rea* and *actus reus* in such situations? The courts appear to disregard this point in order to justify what may be seen as a public policy decision.

HL *Kingston* **[1994] 3 All ER 353, [1994] Crim LR 846**

D claimed his coffee had been spiked by someone who knew that D had paedophilic tendencies and wished to put D into a compromising position for the purposes of blackmail. D was then shown a 15-year-old boy who had been drugged. D indecently assaulted the boy.

(1) Where D has the required *mens rea* for an offence then he cannot use the defence of involuntary intoxication. This is so even though the involuntary intoxication caused him to lose control or become less inhibited.
(2) Where involuntary intoxication causes lack of *mens rea* then it is a defence.

See the cases of *O'Grady* [1987] 3 All ER 420 and *Richardson and Irwin* [1999] Crim LR 494 on intoxication and mistake at **10.1.1**.

CHAPTER 9

DURESS AND NECESSITY

DURESS
DPP for NI v Lynch (1975)
Duress is where D's will is overborne by threats of death or serious injury
Howe (1987)
The defence is not available for murder
Valderrama-Vega (1985)
There must be threats of death or serious injury but a combination of these and other threats can be considered
Hudson and Taylor (1971)
The threat has to be present and immediate
Abdul-Hussain (1999)
(1) The threat must be imminent but it need not be immediate.
(2) The response to a threat need not be spontaneous.
Graham (1982)
(1) D must have acted as he did because of threats of death or serious injury (subjective)
(2) a sober person of reasonable firmness, sharing the characteristics of D, would have responded in the same way (objective)
Hasan (formerly Z) (2005)
The defence is not available where D has voluntarily associated with criminals whom he foresaw or ought reasonably to have foreseen might compel him to act through threats

DURESS AND NECESSITY

DURESS OF CIRCUMSTANCES
Willer (1986)
Threats from circumstances can form the basis of the defence of duress
Martin (1989)
The same principles for duress by threats set out in *Graham* (1982) apply to duress of circumstances
Pommell (1995)
The defence of duress of circumstances is available to the same range of offences as the defence of duress by threats

NECESSITY
Dudley and Stephens (1884)
Necessity is not a defence to murder
Re A (2000)
Necessity is choosing the lesser of two evils to avoid greater harm.

9.1 Duress

DPP for Northern Ireland v Lynch
[1975] 1 All ER 913, (1975) 61 Cr App R 6

D was ordered by M, a terrorist gunman, to drive M and others to a place where they shot and killed a policeman. M was well known as a ruthless killer. D said he feared that if he did not obey M, he, D, would be shot.

Duress is where D's will is overborne by threats of death or serious injury, so that D commits an act which he would not otherwise do.

Howe [1987] 1 All ER 771, (1987) 85 Cr App R 32

D took part in two killings. D claimed that he did this because of threats. The trial judge ruled duress was available for the first killing where D was only a secondary party to the killing, but it was not available for the second killing where D was a principal offender. The House of Lords held that duress was not available as a defence for either murder.

Duress is not available as a defence on a charge of murder. This is so whether D is a principal or a secondary party.

Lord Hailsham LC
'I do not at all accept in relation to the defence of murder it is either good morals, good policy or good law to suggest ... that

the ordinary man of reasonable fortitude is not to be supposed to be capable of heroism if he is asked to take an innocent life rather than sacrifice his own'.

(1) This ruling ignores situations such as a woman motorist being hijacked and forced to act as getaway driver. Lord Griffiths simply dismissed such examples on the basis that it was inconceivable that such person would be prosecuted.

(2) There is an anomaly that duress is not available for murder but is available for a charge under s 18 of the Offences against the Person Act 1861 where the *mens rea* of intention to cause grievous bodily can be the same as for murder.

Gotts [1992] 1 All ER 832, (1992) 94 Cr App R 312.

 Valderrama-Vega [1985] Crim LR 220

D was threatened with disclosure of his homosexuality and put under financial pressure. He was also threatened with death or serious injury. He took part in a scheme to bring cocaine into the UK. The trial judge directed the jury duress was available only if D acted *solely* as a result of the threats of death or serious injury. His conviction was upheld, but the Court of Appeal held that the use of the word solely was wrong.

For the defence of duress to be available there must be threats of death or serious injury. However, if there are other threats together with those of death or serious injury, then the jury can take into account the combination of threats.

Hudson and Taylor [1971] 2 All ER 244, (1971) 56 Cr App R 1

Ds were girls aged 17 and 19 who committd perjury. They claimed they had been threatened by F with being 'cut up'. When they were giving evidence F was in the public gallery. The trial judge ruled that the defence of duress was not available to them as there was no present immediate threat. The threats could not have been carried out there and then. The Court of Appeal quashed their convictions.

(1) Although the threat had to be 'present and immediate', it was enough that it neutralised the will of D at the time D committed the offence.
(2) In deciding whether D should have sought police protection, or otherwise made the threat ineffective, the jury should have regard to the age and circumstances of D.

This decision was criticised by the House of Lords in *Hasan (formerly Z)* (2005) (see below).

 Abdul-Hussain and others [1999] Crim LR 570

Ds were Shiite Muslims from Iraq who had fled to Sudan. They feared they were going to be returned to Iraq where it was likely they would be tortured and killed. They hi-jacked a plane which eventually landed in England. The judge refused to allow the defence of duress to go to the jury and Ds were convicted. The Court of Appeal quashed the convictions.

(1) The threat must be imminent but it need not be immediate.

(2) The response to a threat need not be spontaneous.

Simon Brown LJ

'If Anne Frank had stolen a car to escape from Amsterdam and been charged with theft, the tenets of English law would not, in our judgment, have denied her a defence of duress of circumstances, on the ground that she should have waited for the Gestapo's knock on the door'.

CA *Graham* [1982] 1 All ER 801, (1982) 74 Cr App R 235

D was a homosexual who lived with his wife and another homosexual man, K. K was violent and bullied D. After both D and K had been drinking heavily, K put a flex around the wife's neck and told D to pull the other end of the flex. D did this for about a minute. The wife died. D claimed he had only held the flex because of his fear of K.

For the defence of duress to be available, there are two tests:

(1) D must have acted as he did because of threats of death or serious injury (subjective);

(2) a sober person of reasonable firmness, sharing the characteristics of D, would have responded in the same way to such threats (objective).

The House of Lords in *Hasan (formerly Z)* (2005) (see below) confirmed the decision in *Graham* that D's belief in the threats must be reasonable and genuine.

  Bowen [1996] 4 All ER 83, [1996] 2 Cr App R 157

D was of low IQ and abnormally suggestible. He was charged with obtaining services by deception and claimed he had been forced to do so by two men on the street who had threatened to petrol-bomb him and his family.

Only certain characteristics can be considered for the objective test. These include categories of persons who are less able to resist pressure: examples are age, possibly sex, pregnancy, serious physical disability, recognised mental illness or psychiatric condition.

Stuart-Smith LJ
'The mere fact that the accused is more pliable, vulnerable, timid or susceptible to threats than a normal person are not characteristics with which it is legitimate to invest the reasonable/ordinary person for the purpose of considering the objective test'.

Sharp [1987] 3 All ER 103, (1987) 85 Cr App R 207

D voluntarily joined two others to commit a robbery. D knew that the others were violent and carried firearms. When he wished to withdraw from the robberies, one of the others threatened to kill him. D then took part in another robbery during which a sub-postmaster was shot dead.

The defence of duress is not available where D voluntarily joins a gang whose members he knows are violent.

The courts have allowed duress to be available as a defence where D has voluntarily joined a non-violent gang, see *Shepherd* (1988) 86 Cr App R 47.

Ali [1995] Crim LR 303; *Baker and Ward* [1999] EWCA Crim 913, [1999] 2 Cr App R 335. The leading case is now *Hasan (formerly Z)* (2005) (see below).

 Hasan (formerly Z) [2005] UKHL 22

D associated with a violent drug dealer, who threatened D and his family unless D burgled a house and stole money from a safe. D, carrying a knife, broke into the house but was unable to open the safe. He was convicted of aggravated burglary. The Court of Appeal allowed his appeal but the House of Lords reinstated his conviction.

The defence of duress is excluded where D voluntarily associates with others who are engaged in criminal activity and he foresaw or ought reasonably to have foreseen the risk of being subjected to any compulsion by threats of violence.

9.2 Duress of circumstances

CA *Willer* (1986) 83 Cr App R 225

D was forced to drive his car on the pavement to escape from a gang of youths who were threatening him. He was convicted of reckless driving but the Court of Appeal quashed the conviction on the basis of duress of circumstances.

Threats from circumstances can form the basis of the defence of duress.

This is the first case in which the Court of Appeal accepted that there could be duress of circumstances. Prior to this a defendant could only put forward the defence of necessity. The judgment in *Willer* stated that D was 'wholly driven by force of circumstance into doing what he did and did not drive the car otherwise than under that form of compulsion, ie under duress'.

CA *Martin* [1989] 1 All ER 652, (1989) 88 Cr App R 343

D, who was disqualified from driving, drove his stepson to

work. He only did this because his wife became hysterical and threatened to commit suicide if he did not drive the boy to work and so prevent him from losing his job.

Duress can arise from objective dangers threatening D or others. The same principles for duress by threats set out in *Graham* (1982) apply to duress of circumstances.

(1) D must have acted as he did because he had good cause to fear that otherwise death or serious injury would result (subjective)
(2) a sober person of reasonable firmness, sharing the characteristics of D, would have responded in the same way to that situation (objective).

CA *Pommell* [1995] 2 Cr App R 607

D was found by police in bed at 8 am with a loaded sub-machine gun. He told police that at about 1 am he had taken it off another man who was going to use 'to do some people some damage'. D said he had intended getting his brother to give the gun into the police that morning. The trial judge ruled that the defence of duress was not available and D was convicted. He appealed to the Court of Appeal who quashed the conviction and sent the case for retrial.

The defence of duress of circumstances is available to the same range of offences as the defence of duress by threats.

9.3 Necessity

 Dudley and Stephens (1884) 14 QBD 273

Ds were shipwrecked with another man and V, a 17-year-old cabin boy, in a small boat about 1600 miles from land. After drifting for 20 days Ds killed and ate the cabin boy. Four days later, they were picked up by a passing ship and on their return to England were convicted of murder. Their claim of necessity to save themselves from dying was rejected.

Necessity did not justify the killing of an innocent victim.

Re A (Conjoined twins) [2000] 4 All ER 961, [2001] Crim LR 400

Conjoined twins were born with one of them having no proper heart or lungs. She was being kept alive by the other twin whose heart circulated blood for both of them. Their parents refused to consent to an operation to separate them. Doctors applied for a declaration that it was lawful to operate to separate the twins, even though the weaker twin would certainly die. The Court of Appeal gave the declaration. In the judgment, one of the points considered was the doctrine of necessity.

Necessity can be distinguished from duress as the actor's mind is not 'irresistibly overborne by external pressures'. Necessity is choosing the lesser of two evils to avoid greater harm.

The requirements set out by Stephens in his Digest were held to be still the law. These state:

1 the act is needed to avoid inevitable and irreparable evil;
2 no more should be done than is reasonably necessary for the purpose to be achieved;
3 the evil inflicted must not be disproportionate to the evil avoided.

CHAPTER 10

MISTAKE, SELF-DEFENCE, CONSENT

MISTAKE
DPP v Morgan (1975)
A mistaken belief must be genuinely held, but the mistake need not be reasonable
Williams (Gladstone) (1987)
D must be judged on the facts as he genuinely believed them to be
B v DPP (2000)
Affirmed that D must be judged on the facts as he genuinely believed them to be
O'Grady (1987)
D is not entitled to rely on a mistake of fact which has been induced by voluntary intoxication

SELF-DEFENCE
Palmer v R (1971)
D may use what force is reasonably necessary in self-defence. The force must not be wholly out of proportion to the threat
Clegg (1995)
The defence is not available if excessive force is used
A-G's Ref (No 2 of 1983) (1984)
Where self-defence is necessary then acts preparatory to it are also lawful

MISTAKE
CONSENT, SELF-DEFENCE

CONSENT
Tabassum (2000)
There must be true consent to the nature and the quality of the act for D to establish a defence of consent
Dica (2004)
Where V is ignorant of D's infection, V is not consenting to the risk of infection
Donovan (1934)
Consent is not available as a defence where actual bodily harm is intended or likely to be caused
A-G's Ref (No 6 of 1980) (1981)
Consent is NOT available as a defence in private fights, but it is available as a defence in properly conducted games and sports
Brown (1993)
Consent is not available as a defence to charges of assault where injury was caused
Jones and others (1986)
It is a defence where D genuinely believes that V has consented to 'rough and undisciplined horseplay'

10.1 Mistake

HL *DPP v Morgan* [1975] 2 All ER 411, (1975) 61 Cr App R 136

D invited friends to have sex with his wife, telling them that she was willing but might simulate reluctance for her own pleasure. In fact, the wife did not consent and struggled and shouted. The men were convicted of rape and D of incitement to rape. The trial judge directed the jury that the men would be guilty of rape if their belief in her consent was not based on reasonable grounds. They appealed.

A mistaken belief must be genuinely held, but the mistake need not be reasonable.

Lord Hailsham
'Since honest belief clearly negatives intent, the reasonableness or otherwise of that belief can only be evidence for or against the view that the belief and, therefore, the intent was actually held'.

CA **Williams (Gladstone)** [1987]
3 All ER 411, (1987) 78 Cr App R 276

D saw V dragging a youth along the street and hitting him. The youth was calling for help. D punched V, believing that V was assaulting the youth. In fact, V was a police officer who had arrested the youth for mugging an old lady. The jury were directed that a mistake would only be relevant if it were a reasonable mistake. D's appeal was upheld and his conviction quashed.

 D must be judged on the facts as he genuinely believed them to be. The belief does not have to be reasonable.

 Lord Lane
'The reasonableness or unreasonableness of D's belief is material to the question of whether the belief was held by D at all. If the belief was in fact held its unreasonableness, so far as guilt or innocence is concerned, is neither here nor there'.

 Beckford v R [1987] 3 All ER 425 Privy Council.

 B v DPP [2000] I All ER 823, [2000] 2 Cr App R 65

D, a boy of 15, sat next to a 13-year-old girl on a bus and repeatedly asked her to perform oral sex. He believed that the girl was 14 or over. D was charged with inciting a child under 14 to commit an act of gross indecency, under s 1(1) of the Indecency with Children Act 1960. The magistrates ruled that the offence was one of strict liability. D's conviction was quashed on appeal.

The House of Lords affirmed the decision in *Williams (Gladstone)* (see above). D is to be judged on the facts as he genuinely believed them to be.

O'Grady [1987] 3 All ER 420, (1987) 85 Cr App R 315

D and V drank a large amount of alcohol and then fell asleep at V's home. D woke up to find V attacking him. D hit back and then went to sleep again. In the morning he discovered that V was dead. He was convicted of manslaughter.

Where D relies on the defence of self-defence, he is not entitled to rely on a mistake of fact which has been induced by voluntary intoxication.

10.2 Self-defence

 Palmer v R [1971] 1 All ER 1077, (1971) 55 Cr App R 223

D had gone with other men to buy drugs. A dispute arose and D and the others left without paying. They were chased and D shot and killed one of the chasers. He claimed that he was acting in self-defence but he was convicted of murder.

D may use what force is reasonably necessary in self-defence. The force must not be wholly out of proportion to the threat.

Lord Morris
'It is both good law and good sense that a man who is attacked may defend himself, but [he] may only do what is reasonably necessary. But everything will depend on the

particular facts and the circumstances … If there has been an attack so that defence is reasonably necessary, it will be recognised that a person defending himself cannot weigh to a nicety the exact measure of his necessary defensive action. If a jury thought that in a moment of unexpected anguish a person attacked had only done what he honestly and instinctively thought was necessary that would be most potent evidence that only reasonable defensive action had been taken'.

HL *Clegg* [1995] 1 All ER 334

D was a soldier on duty at a checkpoint in Northern Ireland. A car failed to stop at the checkpoint and D shouted at the driver to stop it. D fired four shots at the car. One of the shots killed a passenger in the car. The evidence was that the car was some 50 yards past the checkpoint by the time the fatal shot was fired. D was convicted of murder.

Where excessive force is used, then the defence of self-defence is not available.

CA *Attorney-General's Reference* (No 2 of 1983) [1984] QB 456

D's shop had been attacked by rioters. Worried that there would be further attacks, he made petrol bombs. D was charged with possessing an explosive substance in circumstances as to give rise to a reasonable suspicion that he did not have it for a lawful purpose. He pleaded that he had it in self-defence. He was acquitted and the point of law referred to the Court of Appeal.

Where self-defence is necessary then acts preparatory to it are also lawful.

The law on self-defence also includes defence of another person. It also overlaps with s 3 of the Criminal Law Act 1967 on force used in the prevention of crime.

10.3 Consent

CA *Tabassum* [2000] Crim LR 686, [2000] 2 Cr App R 328

Three women allowed D to touch their breasts for the purpose of preparing a database in relation to breast cancer. They thought D was medically qualified or trained and, because of this, they consented to the touching. D was not medically trained. He was convicted of indecent assault.

There must be true consent to the nature and the quality of the act for D to establish a defence of consent.

CA *Dica* [2004] EWCA Crim 1103

D, who knew he was HIV positive, had relationships with two women. They had unprotected sex with him and both became infected. They claimed that they did not know he was HIV positive and that if they had they would not have agreed to unprotected sex. The judge did not allow the issue of consent to go to the jury, so the Court of Appeal quashed the conviction but ordered a retrial.

The consent must be informed and willing to provide a defence.

Konzani [2005] Cr App Rep 14.

CA *Donovan* **[1934] All ER 207, (1934) 25 Cr App R 1**

D caned a 17-year-old girl for sexual gratification. This caused bruising and he was convicted of indecent assault and a common assault. D appealed on the basis that V had consented to the act. His conviction was quashed.

In general consent is not available as a defence where actual bodily harm is intended or likely to be caused. There are public policy exceptions which include 'mutual manly contests' and 'rough and undisciplined sport or play where there is no anger and no intention to cause bodily harm'.

CA *Attorney-General's Reference (No 6 of 1980)*
[1981] 2 All ER 1057, (1981) 73 Cr App R 63

Two men who had quarrelled agreed to settle their differences by a fight in the street. One of them suffered a bleeding nose and bruises.

Consent is not available as a defence in private fights. Consent is available as a defence to properly conducted games and sports.

Lord Lane CJ

'It is not in the public interest that people should try to cause, or should cause, each other bodily harm for no good reason. Minor struggles are another matter. So ... it is immaterial whether the act occurs in private or public: it is an assault if actual bodily harm is intended and/or caused. This means that most fights will be unlawful regardless of consent. Nothing which we have said is intended to cast doubt upon the accepted legality of properly conducted games and sports ... reasonable surgical interference, dangerous exhibitions, etc.'

 Brown [1993] 2 All ER 75, (1993) 97 Cr App R 44

Five men in a group of consenting adult sado–masochists were convicted of offences of assault causing actual bodily harm (s 47 Offences Against the Person Act 1861) and malicious wounding (s 20 Offences Against the Person Act 1861). They had carried out acts which included applying stinging nettles to the genital area and inserting map pins or fish hooks into the penises of each other. All the victims had consented and none had needed medical attention.

Consent was not available as a defence to charges of assault where injury was caused, even though the acts were between adults in private and did not result in serious bodily injury.

Wilson [1996] 3 WLR 125, [1996] 2 Cr App R 241

A husband used a heated butter knife to brand his initials on his wife's buttocks, at her request. The wife's burns became infected and she needed medical treatment. He was convicted of assault causing actual bodily harm (s 47 Offences Against the Person Act 1861) but on appeal the Court of Appeal quashed the conviction.

Consensual activity between husband and wife should not normally be criminalised.

 Jones and others (1986) 83 Cr App R 375

The victims, two boys aged 14 and 15, were tossed in the air by the defendants who were older boys. One V suffered a broken arm and the other a ruptured spleen. Ds' convictions were quashed as the judge did not allow the issue of mistaken belief (that Vs had consented to the tossing) to go to the jury.

There is no assault where D genuinely believes that V has consented to 'rough and undisciplined horseplay'. It is irrelevant whether that belief is reasonable or not.

HOMICIDE

MENS REA FOR MURDER
Vickers (1957)
Intention to cause grievous bodily harm is sufficient for the *mens rea* of murder
Moloney (1985)
Foresight of consequences is only evidence from which the intention for murder may be found
Woollin (1998)
The jury are not entitled to *find* the necessary intention unless they feel sure that death or serious bodily harm was a virtual certainty as a result of D's act and that D realised this

MURDER

PARTIAL DEFENCES

DIMINISHED RESPONSIBILITY
Byrne (1960)
'Abnormality of mind' is wide enough to cover perception, ability to form rational judgment and to exercise willpower
Seers (1984)
Comparison with insanity is not helpful: substantial means more than trivial but not total or absolute impairment
Dietschmann (2003)
The abnormality does not have to be the sole cause of D's acts in doing the killing
Tandy (1989)
Intoxication is a defence only if D can show that his brain has been injured or that the drinking was involuntary

PROVOCATION
Duffy (1949)
D must suffer a sudden loss of self-control
Thornton (No 2) (1996)
A minor incident can be the last straw
Camplin (1978)
D is expected to have the power of self-control of a reasonable person of D's age and sex
Other characteristics affecting the gravity of the provocation are taken into account
Morhall (1995)
Disreputable characteristics are relevant to the gravity of the provocation
Smith (Morgan James) (2000)
Are the circumstances sufficiently excusable to allow the defence
A-G v Holley (2005)
D is to be judged by the standard of a person having ordinary powers of self-control

Attorney-General's Reference (No 3 of 1994)
[1997] 3 All ER 936, [1998] 1 Cr App R 91

See **3.4**.

A foetus is not a person and there is no liability for murder or manslaughter for killing a foetus. However, where the foetus suffers an attack while in the womb, is afterwards born as a living child, but then dies as a result of the attack on it when it was a foetus, D can be liable for murder or manslaughter depending on his intention.

11.1 *Mens rea* for murder

Vickers [1957] 2 All ER 741, (1957) 41 Cr App R 189

D broke into the cellar of a local sweet shop. He was interrupted by the old lady who ran the shop. D hit her several blows with his fists and kicked her once in the head. She died as a result of her injuries. The Court of Appeal upheld his conviction for murder.

An intention to cause grievous bodily harm is sufficient for the *mens rea* of murder. It does not have to be proved that D had the intention to kill.

The old common law definition of murder states that the *mens rea* of murder is 'malice aforethought express or implied'.

Express malice is the intention to kill: implied malice is the intention to cause grievous bodily harm.

In 2005 the Law Commission published a consultation paper on murder which proposed that only an intention to kill would be sufficient for first tier murder.

HL *Moloney* [1985] 1 All ER 1025, (1985) 81 Cr App R 93

See **3.1**.

Foresight by D that death or grievous bodily harm is virtually certain to result as the result of D's acts or omissions is evidence from which the required intention for murder can be found.

HL *Woollin* [1998] 4 All ER 103, [1999] 1 Cr App R 8

See **3.1**.

The model direction to a jury considering foresight of consequences should be:

'the jury should be directed that they are not entitled to *find* the necessary intention unless they feel sure that death or serious bodily harm was a virtual certainty (barring some unforeseen intervention) as a result of D's actions and that D appreciated that such was the case.'

Hancock and Shankland [1986] 1 All ER 641 and *Nedrick*
[1986] 3 All ER 1: see **3.1**.

11.2 Diminished responsibility

CCA *Byrne* [1960] 3 All ER 1, (1960) 44 Cr App R 246

D was a sexual psychopath who strangled a young
woman and then mutilated her body. The medical
evidence was that, because of his condition, he was
unable to control his perverted desires. He was
convicted of murder but the Court of Appeal
quashed the conviction and substituted a
conviction for manslaughter.

The phrase 'abnormality of mind' in the Homicide
Act 1957 is wide enough to cover:

- the perception of physical acts and matters;
- the ability to form a rational judgement as to
  whether an act is right or wrong; and
- the ability to exercise willpower to control
  physical acts in accordance with that rational
  judgement.

 CA *Seers* (1984) 79 Cr App R 261

D, who was suffering from chronic reactive depression, killed
his wife. The trial judge had directed the jury that the defence
was only available to those who were 'partially insane' or 'on

the borderline of insanity'. The Court of Appeal quashed his
conviction for murder and substituted one for manslaughter.

(1) Comparisons with insanity are not helpful and should
be avoided.
(2) Substantial means more than trivial but not total or
absolute impairment.

HL *Dietschmann* [2003] UKHL 10

D, who was suffering from an adjustment disorder in the form
of depressed grief reaction to the death of his aunt, was upset
by V's disrespectful behaviour. D killed V by repeatedly
kicking him and stamping on him. D had also drunk a large
amount of alcohol before the killing. He was convicted. The
House of Lords allowed his appeal.

The abnormality does not have to be the sole cause of D's acts
in doing the killing. Even if D would not have killed if he had
not taken the drink, the causative effect of the drink does not
necessarily prevent an abnormality of mind from substantially
impairing his mental responsibility.

Gittens [1984] 3 WLR 327.

CA *Tandy* [1989] 1 All ER 267, (1989) 87 Cr App R 45

Mrs Tandy had been an alcoholic for a number of years. One day she drank nearly a whole bottle of vodka. That evening she told her mother that her (Tandy's) second husband had sexually interfered with her 11-year-old daughter. She then strangled her daughter. The trial judge told the jury to decide whether Tandy was suffering from an abnormality of mind as a direct result of her alcoholism or whether she was just drunk. She was convicted and the Court of Appeal upheld her conviction.

Intoxication can only provide a defence under diminished responsibility if D can show that D's brain has been injured by the consumption of alcohol, or that the drinking was involuntary.

11.3 Provocation

 CCA *Duffy* [1949] 1 All ER 932

D, who was an abused wife, had a quarrel with her husband. She then left the room and changed her clothes. When her husband was in bed she attacked him with a hammer and a hatchet. D's conviction for murder was upheld.

Provocation is only available as a defence where D suffers a sudden loss of self-control.

Devlin J

'Provocation is some act, or series of acts done (or words spoken) … which would cause in any reasonable person, and actually causes in the accused, a sudden and temporary loss of self-control, rendering the accused so subject to passion as to make him or her for the moment not master of his or her own mind'.

This case was decided prior to the enactment of the Homicide Act 1957. However, the definition given by Devlin J has been accepted in cases decided since the Act became law.

D's actions were held not to come within the definition in Devlin's judgment. However, in the later case of *Thornton* (see below), it was accepted that there can be a slow burn reaction leading to a sudden loss of self-control.

 Thornton (No 2) [1996] 1 WLR 1174, [1996] 2 Cr App R 108

D's husband was jealous and possessive and physically abused her. He also drank heavily. One night her husband threatened that he would kill her when she was asleep. D then went into the kitchen and sharpened a bread knife. She returned to the living room and stabbed her husband in the stomach. She was convicted of murder. The Court of Appeal quashed the conviction and order a re-trial at which the jury acquitted D.

It is accepted that there can be a sudden loss of self-control triggered by a minor incident. In other words it is the last straw which sparks the killing. This comes within the concept of a sudden loss of self-control.

HL *Camplin*
[1978] AC 705, (1978) 67 Cr App R 14

 D was a 15-year-old boy who had been sexually abused by an older man who had then laughed at him. D reacted to this by hitting the man over the head with a chapatti pan. At the trial the judge directed the jury to ignore the boy's age and consider what effect the provocation would have had on the reasonable adult and he was convicted of murder. The House of Lords allowed his appeal and substituted a conviction for manslaughter.

 There are two points to be considered for the reasonable man test in s 3 of the Homicide Act 1957. These are:

1 for the purposes of self-control the level is the power of self-control to be expected from a person of the age and sex of D;

2 for the gravity of the provocation the reasonable man shares such of D's characteristics as the jury think would affect the gravity to D.

 Lord Diplock
'The reasonable man is a person having the power of self-control to be expected of an ordinary person of the sex and age of the accused, but in

> other respects sharing such of the accused's
> characteristics as they think would affect the
> gravity of the provocation to him; and that the
> question is not merely whether such a person
> would in like circumstances be provoked to lose
> his self-control but whether he would react to the
> provocation as the accused did'.

 Morhall [1995] 3 All ER 659, [1995] 2 Cr App R 502

D was a glue-sniffer who was being nagged about this by V. D
stabbed V and was convicted of murder. The House of Lords
quashed his conviction and substituted one of manslaughter.

Even disreputable characteristics such as glue-sniffing can be
taken into account when considering the gravity of the
provocation to D.

 Smith (Morgan James) [2000] 4 All ER 289, [2001] 1 Cr App R 31

During an argument with a friend about whether the friend
had stolen some tools belonging to D, D picked up a kitchen
knife and stabbed the victim. There was evidence that D was
suffering from a depressive illness which might have reduced
his threshold for reacting to provocation. The trial judge ruled
that this characteristic was not relevant to the reasonable man's
loss of self-control. His conviction for murder was quashed.

The question is whether in all the circumstances the jury consider that the defendant's loss of self-control was excusable and this will be judged by reference to how a person, in his position, exercising ordinary powers of self-control would have behaved. The objective element of the test for provocation is whether the jury think that the circumstances were such as to make the loss of self-control sufficiently excusable to reduce the gravity of the offence from murder to manslaughter.

PC *Attorney-General for Jersey v Holley* [2005] UKPC 23

D was an alcoholic who had been drinking heavily. He claimed that his long-standing girlfriend told him she had had sex with another man and taunted him. He struck her with an axe he was using to chop wood.

D is to be judged by the standard of a person having ordinary powers of self-control.

This decision by the Privy Council is not binding on the courts in England and Wales. The majority (six of a panel of nine) held that the decision in *Smith (Morgan James)* (2000) (see above) was wrong. However, in *Mohammed* [2005] EWCA Crim 1880 the Court of Appeal followed *Holley* rather than the decision in *Smith (Morgan James)*.

> **UNLAWFUL ACT MANSLAUGHTER**
> *Lowe* (1973)
> An omission is not sufficient for the *actus reus* of unlawful act manslaughter
> *Church* (1965)
> The unlawful act must be one which a sober and reasonable person would recognise put V at risk of some harm
> *Goodfellow* (1986)
> The unlawful act can be aimed at property, provided it puts people at the risk of harm
> *Dawson* (1985)
> Causing fear is not a dangerous act unless D knows V is at risk of injury from the fear
> *DPP v Newbury and Jones* (1976)
> D need only have the *mens rea* for the unlawful act: there is no need to prove that D foresaw harm

INVOLUNTARY MANSLAUGHTER

> **GROSS NEGLIGENCE MANSLAUGHTER**
> *Bateman* (1925)
> Gross negligence is conduct which goes so far beyond the civil tort of negligence so as to be considered criminal
> *Adomako* (1994)
> There must be a duty of care, breach of that duty which causes V's death and the negligence must be so bad in all the circumstances as to amount to a criminal act or omission
> *Khan and Khan* (1998)
> The categories of duty of care can be extended on a case by case basis
> *Wacker* (2003)
> Even though V is involved with D in a criminal act, D can still owe V a duty of care

11.4 Unlawful act manslaughter

Lowe [1973] 1 All ER 805, (1973) 57 Cr App R 365

D was convicted of wilfully neglecting his baby son and of his manslaughter. The Court of Appeal quashed the conviction for manslaughter because the finding of wilful neglect involved a failure to act and this could not support a conviction for unlawful act manslaughter.

An omission is not sufficient for the *actus reus* of unlawful act manslaughter.

CCA *Church* [1965] 2 All ER 72, (1965) 49 Cr App R 206

D had a fight with a woman and knocked her out. He tried for half an hour, unsuccessfully, to bring her round. He thought she was dead and pushed her into a river. In fact, she was alive when she entered the river but died through drowning.

The unlawful act must be one which a sober and reasonable person would recognise put V at risk of some harm.

Edmund Davies J
'The unlawful act must be such as all sober and reasonable people would inevitably recognise must subject the other person to, at least, the risk of some harm resulting therefrom, albeit not serious harm'.

CA *Goodfellow* (1986) 83 Cr App R 23

D decided to set fire to his council flat so that the council would have to re-house him. The fire got out of control and his wife, son and another woman died in the fire. He was convicted of manslaughter and appealed. The Court of Appeal upheld the conviction because all the elements of unlawful act manslaughter were present.

Even though the unlawful act was aimed at property, the elements of unlawful act manslaughter were present:

- the act was committed intentionally;
- it was unlawful;
- reasonable people would recognise that it might cause some harm to another person;
- the act caused the death.

 CA *Dawson* (1985) 81 Cr App R 150

Three defendants attempted to rob a petrol station. They were masked and armed with pickaxe handles. The petrol station attendant pressed the alarm and the robbers fled. The attendant, who had a serious heart condition, then died from a heart attack. Ds' convictions were quashed.

The act must be a one likely to harm some harm in the eyes of reasonable people. Frightening a man of 60 would not normally be expected to cause harm and so was not a dangerous act for unlawful act manslaughter.

 CA *Watson* [1989] 2 All ER 865, (1989) 89 Cr App R 211

Two defendants threw a brick through the window of a house and got into it intending to steal property. The occupier was a frail 87-year-old man who heard the noise and came to investigate what had happened. The two defendants physically abused him and then left. The man died of a heart attack 90 minutes later.

Where a reasonable person would be aware of V's frailty and the risk of harm to him, then the unlawful act is dangerous within the *Church* test.

HL

DPP v Newbury and Jones
[1976] 2 All ER 365, (1976) 62 Cr App R 291

The defendants were two teenage boys who pushed a piece of paving stone from a bridge on to a railway line as a train was approaching. The stone hit the train and killed the guard. They were convicted of manslaughter.

It was not necessary to prove that the defendant foresaw any harm from his act. The defendant could be convicted provided the unlawful act was dangerous and the defendant had the necessary *mens rea* for that act.

Attorney-General's Reference (No 2 of 1999) [2000] 3 All ER 187.

CA *Dias* [2002] 2 Cr App R 5

D prepared a syringe of heroin and gave it to V who injected himself. D then injected himself. When D had recovered from the effects of the heroin he realised that V was very ill. He asked a passer-by to call an ambulance and then left the scene. V was taken to hospital but died.

Self-injection of a Class A drug is not an unlawful act, so it cannot be the basis for a conviction of unlawful act manslaughter.

The court left open the question as to whether there might be a conviction in the future on the basis that there was an unlawful act of administering a noxious substance under s 23 of the Offences Against the Person Act 1861.

CA *Rogers* [2003] 2 Cr App R 10

D had helped V to inject himself with heroin by holding his belt round V's arm as a tourniquet to make it easier for V to find the vein to inject.

Applying a tourniquet was part of the act of injecting and so D had committed the unlawful act of administering a noxious substance under s 23 of the Offences Against the Person Act 1861.

11.5 Gross negligence manslaughter

CCA *Bateman* [1925] All ER 45, (1925) 19 Cr App R 8

D, a doctor, attended V for the birth of her child at her home, during which part of V's uterus came away. D did not send V to hospital for five days, and she later died. D's conviction was quashed on the basis that he had acted as any competent doctor would have done. He had not been grossly negligent.

Gross negligence is conduct which goes so far beyond the civil tort of negligence so as to be considered criminal.

Lord Hewart
'The facts must be such that, in the opinion of the jury, the negligence of the accused went beyond a mere matter of compensation between subjects and showed such disregard for the life and safety of others as to amount to a crime against the State and conduct deserving of punishment'.

HL *Adomako*
[1994] 3 All ER 79

D was an anaesthetist. He failed to notice that during an operation one of the tubes supplying oxygen to a patient became disconnected. The lack of oxygen caused the patient to suffered a heart attack and brain damage. As a result, the patient died six months later.

(1) The elements of gross negligence manslaughter are:
  • the existence of a duty of care towards the victim;
  • a breach of that duty if care which causes death;
  • gross negligence which the jury considers to be criminal.

(2) To be considered gross negligence, the conduct of the defendant must be so bad in all the circumstances and having regard to the

> risk of death involved, as to amount, in the
> judgment of the jury, to a criminal act or
> omission.
>
> **Lord Mackay**
> 'The ordinary principles of the law of negligence
> apply to ascertain whether or not the defendant
> has been in breach of a duty of care towards the
> victim. ... The jury will have to consider whether
> the extent to which the defendant's conduct
> departed from the proper standard of care
> incumbent upon him involving as it must have
> done a risk of death ..., was such that it should be
> judged criminal'.

CA *Khan and Khan* [1998] Crim LR 830

The two defendants had supplied heroin to a new user who
took it in their presence and then collapsed. They left her
alone and by the time they returned to the flat she had died.
Their conviction for unlawful act manslaughter was quashed
but the Court of Appeal thought there could be a duty to
summon medical assistance in certain circumstances.

The categories of duty of care can be extended on a case-by-
case basis.

CA *Wacker* [2003] 1 Cr App R 22

D agreed to bring 60 illegal immigrants into England. They

were put in the back of his lorry for a cross-channel ferry crossing. The only air into the lorry was through a small vent and it was agreed that this vent should be closed at certain times to prevent the immigrants being discovered. D closed the vent before boarding the ferry. The crossing took an hour longer than usual and at Dover the Customs officers found 58 of the immigrants were dead.

Although no action could arise in a civil case because the victims were involved in criminal behaviour, it was still possible for there to be a breach of a duty of care in a criminal case.

Misra and another
[2004] UKCA Crim 2375, [2005] 1 Cr App R 21

The two defendants were senior house doctors responsible for the post operative care of V. They failed to identify and treat V for an infection which occurred after the operation. V died from the infection.

The test in gross negligence manslaughter involves consideration of the risk of death. It is not sufficient to show a risk of bodily injury or injury to health.

The defendants had appealed on the basis that the elements of gross negligence manslaughter were uncertain and so breached Article 7 of the European Convention on Human Rights. The Court of Appeal held that *Adomako* had clearly laid down the elements, so there was no breach of Article 7.

CHAPTER 12

ASSAULTS

ASSAULT AND BATTERY
Ireland (1998): *Smith v Chief Superintendent of Woking* (1983)
Putting V in fear of the possibility of immediate force is sufficient
Collins v Wilcock (1984)
The slightest physical restraint can be battery
DPP v Santa-Bermudez (2003)
An omission is sufficient for the *actus reus*
Mens rea
Venna (1974)
subjective reckless is sufficient

ASSAULT OCCASIONING ABH (s 47)
Actual bodily harm
T v DPP (2003)
Momentary loss of consciousness can be ABH
Chan Fook (1994)
Psychiatric injury can be ABH
Mens rea
Savage (1991)
There is no need to prove any intention to injury

ASSAULTS

ACTUS REUS **OF s 20 AND s 18 OAPA 1861**
Burstow (1997)
It is not necessary to prove an asault for either 'inflict' or 'cause'
Martin (1881)
An indirect act is sufficient for s 20
JCC v Eisenhower (1983)
There must be a cut of the external skin to constitute a wound
DPP v Smith (1961)
GBH means really serious harm
Bollam (2004)
The age and health of the victim must be considered in deciding the seriousness

MENS REA **OF s 20 AND s 18**
Mowatt (1967)
'Maliciously' for s 20 means an intention to injure or taking the risk of some injury
Parmenter (1991)
Affirmed *Mowatt* – there is no need for D to realise that serious injury could be caused
Morrison (1989)
In s 18 where the ulterior intent is to resist arrest, maliciously means taking the risk of injuring V

12.1 Assault and battery

 Ireland [1997] 4 All ER 225, [1998] 1 Cr App R 177

D made a large number of silent telephone calls to three women. This caused them psychiatric injury. He was convicted of an assault occasioning actual bodily harm under s 47 of the Offences Against the Person Act 1861.

It was held that *making* telephone calls, even silent ones, can amount to an assault.

Lord Steyn
'Take now the case of the silent caller. He intends by his silence to cause fear and he is so understood. The victim is assailed by uncertainty about his intentions. Fear may dominate her emotions, and it may be the fear that the caller's arrival at her door may be imminent. She may fear the *possibility* of immediate personal violence'.

Constanza [1997] Crim LR 576 CA.

Such cases could now also be charged under the Protection from Harassment Act 1997. Section 4 of this Act defines harassment as 'causing another to fear, on at least two occasions, that violence will be used against him'.

Smith v Chief Superintendent of Woking Police Station
[1983] Crim LR 323

D got into a garden and looked through a woman's ground floor bedroom window at about 11 pm. She was in her nightclothes and was terrified. D was convicted of being on enclosed premises for an unlawful purpose (ie an assault).

Although D was outside the house and no attack could be made at that immediate moment, the court held that his conduct was an assault. The woman feared some immediate violence and this was sufficient the purposes of an assault.

 Collins v Wilcock
[1984] 3 All ER 374 (1984) 79 Cr App Rep 229

Two police officers saw two women apparently soliciting for the purposes of prostitution. They asked D to get into the police car for questioning but she refused and walked away. One of the officers walked after her to try to find out her identity. She refused to speak to the officer and again walked away. The officer then took hold of her by the arm to prevent her leaving. D became abusive and scratched the officer's arm. Her conviction of assaulting a police officer in the execution of his duty was quashed on the basis that the officer was not acting in the execution of his duty, but was acting unlawfully by holding the defendant's arm. The court held that the officer had committed a battery and the defendant was entitled to free herself.

Touching a person to get his attention is acceptable provided that only necessary physical contact is used; physical restraint is not acceptable and will be a battery unless there is consent to the touching.

Goff LJ
'The fundamental principle ... is that every person's body is inviolate. It has long been established that any touching of another person, however slight, may amount to battery'.

DPP v Santa-Bermudez [2003] EWHC 2908

A police woman, before searching the defendant's pockets, asked him if he had any needles or other sharp objects on him. The defendant said 'no', but when the police officer put her hand in his pocket she was injured by a needle which caused bleeding. He was convicted of assault occasioning actual bodily harm under s 47 Offences against the Person Act 1861.

Failure to tell the police officer of the needle could amount to the *actus reus* for the purposes of an assault causing actual bodily harm.

Tuberville v Savage (1669) 1 Mod Rep 3

D placed his hand on the hilt of his sword and said to V: 'If it were not assize-time, I would not take such language from you.' D was held not guilty of assault.

The accompanying words made it clear that no violence was going to be used. There was no reason for V to fear immediate force, so there was no assault.

 CCR *Light* [1843–60] All ER 934

D raised a sword above his wife's head, telling her: 'Were it not for the bloody policeman outside, I would split your head open.' D was held guilty of assault.

There was an assault as, despite the words, V had cause to fear immediate force in these circumstances.

These two cases are difficult to reconcile, but it can be argued that in *Tuberville v Savage* D had not drawn his sword, whereas, in *Light*, D had raised the sword the above V's head.

 CA *Venna* [1976] QB 421, (1976) 61 Cr App R 310

D and others were causing a disturbance in the street. The police were sent for. When the police tried to arrest D, he kicked out, causing a fracture to a small bone in the officer's hand. D was convicted of assault occasioning actual bodily harm.

Subjective recklessness was sufficient for the *mens rea* of battery.

James LJ

'We see no reason in logic or in law why a person who recklessly applies physical force to the person of another should be outside the criminal law of assault'.

12.2 Section 47 OAPA 1861

OAPA 1861, s 47

Whosoever shall be convicted on indictment of any assault occasioning actual bodily harm shall be liable to imprisonment for not more than five years.

This means that the *actus reus* for s 47 is any assault or battery (see **12.1**).

T v DPP [2003] Crim LR 622

D and a group of other youths chased V. V fell to the ground and saw D coming towards him. V covered his head with his arms and was kicked. He momentarily lost consciousness and remembered nothing until being woken by a police officer. D was convicted of assault occasioning actual bodily harm.

Momentary loss of consciousness could be actual bodily harm. 'Harm' was a synonym for injury. 'Actual' indicated that the injury should not be so trivial as to be wholly insignificant. Loss of consciousness fell within the meaning of actual bodily harm.

Chan Fook [1994] 2 All ER 552, (1994) 99 Cr App R 147

D thought that V had stolen his fiancée's ring. D dragged V upstairs and locked him in a second-floor room. V tried to escape but was injured when he fell to the ground. At D's trial on a s 47 charge it was claimed that V had suffered trauma before the escape bid and that this amounted to ABH. The judge directed the jury that a hysterical or nervous condition was capable of being ABH. D was convicted but the Court of Appeal quashed the conviction.

Psychiatric injury is capable of amounting to actual bodily harm but 'mere emotions such as fear, distress or panic' do not amount to ABH.

Hobhouse LJ
'The body of the victim includes all parts of his body, including his organs, his nervous system and his brain. Bodily injury therefore may include injury to any of those parts of his body responsible for his mental and other faculties'.

- *Ireland* [1997] 4 All ER 225: see **10.1.1**.
- *Burstow* [1997] 4 All ER 225: see **10.3.1**.

HL *Savage*
[1991] 4 All ER 698, (1991) 94 Cr App R 193

D threw beer over another woman in a pub. In doing this the glass slipped from D's hand and V's hand was cut by the glass. D said that she had only intended to throw beer over the woman. D had not intended her to be injured, nor had she realised that there was a risk of injury. She was convicted of a s 20 offence but the Court of Appeal quashed that and substituted a conviction under s 47 (assault occasioning actual bodily harm). She appealed against this to the House of Lords. The Law Lords dismissed her appeal.

Intention to apply unlawful force is sufficient for the *mens rea* of a s 47 offence. The prosecution need not prove that D intended or was reckless as to any injury.

Lord Ackner
'The verdict of assault occasioning actual bodily harm may be returned upon proof of an assault together with proof of the fact that actual bodily harm was occasioned by the assault. The prosecution is not obliged to prove that the defendant intended to cause some actual bodily harm or was reckless as to whether such harm would be caused'.

12.3 Sections 20 and 18 OAPA 1861

OAPA 1861, s 20

Whosoever shall unlawfully and maliciously wound or inflict and grievous bodily harm upon any other person, either with or without a weapon or instrument, shall be guilty of an offence ...

OAPA 1861, s 18

Whosoever shall unlawfully and maliciously by any means whatsoever wound or caused grievous bodily harm to any other person, with intent to do some grievous bodily harm, or with intent to resist or prevent the lawful apprehension or detainer of any person shall be guilty ... of an offence.

CCR *Martin* (1881) 8 QBD 54

D placed an iron bar across the doorway of a theatre. He then switched off the lights and yelled 'fire'. In the panic which followed several of the audience were injured when they were trapped and unable to open the door. Martin was convicted of an offence under s 20 OAPA 1861.

Grievous bodily harm can be 'inflicted' for the purposes of s 20 through an indirect act such as a booby trap.

HL *Burstow*
[1997] 4 All ER 225, [1998] 1 Cr App R 177

D carried out an eight-month campaign of harassment against a woman with whom he had had a brief relationship some three years earlier. The harassment consisted of both silent and abusive telephone calls, hate mail and stalking. This caused V to suffer from severe depression.

It was decided that 'inflict' does not require a technical assault or a battery. This decision means that there now appears to be little, if any, difference in the *actus reus* of the offences under s 20 ('causing') and s 18 ('inflicting').

Lord Hope
'I would add that there is this difference, the word "inflict" implies that the consequence of the act is something which the victim is likely to find unpleasant or harmful. The relationship between cause and effect, when the word "cause" is used, is neutral. It may embrace pleasure as well as pain. The relationship when the word "inflict" is used is more precise, because it invariably implies detriment to the victim of some kind'.

The wording of the 1861 Act is unclear and the offences do not form a coherent range. The Law Commission set out a draft Bill proposing reform of the law, but this has never been enacted.

Serious psychiatric injury can amount to grievous bodily harm. This case was heard together with *Ireland* (see **12.1.1**).

Mowatt [1967] 3 All ER 47, (1967) 51 Cr App R 402

Either D or his friend had taken £5 from V's pocket. V realised this and seized D. D hit out at V, allegedly in self-defence, punching him repeatedly until V was nearly unconscious. D was convicted under s 20 OAPA 1861. The Court of Appeal upheld his conviction.

For s 20 there is no need to prove that D had intention to cause serious injury or that he realised there was a risk of serious injury. It is sufficient to prove that D foresaw that some harm might result.

Diplock LJ

'The word "maliciously" does import ... an awareness that his act may have the consequence of causing some physical harm to some other person ... It is quite unnecessary that the accused should have foreseen that his unlawful act might cause physical harm of the gravity described in [s 20], ie a wound or serious physical injury. It is enough that he should have foreseen that some physical harm to some person, albeit of a minor character might result'.

The judgment refers only to physical harm. However, since *Mowatt* was decided, it has been established that serious psychiatric injury also comes within the meaning of grievous bodily harm. So D has the required *mens* rea if he realizes that his acts might cause serious psychiatric injury to V.

Parmenter [1991] 4 All ER 698, (1991) 94 Cr App R 193

D injured his three-month-old baby when he threw the child in the air and caught him. D said that he often done this with slightly older children and did not realise that there was risk of any injury. He was convicted of an offence under s 20. The House of Lords quashed this conviction but substituted a conviction for assault occasioning actual bodily harm under s 47.

The word 'maliciously' in s 20 means only that D must be aware that some injury might be caused by his act.

 Morrison (1989) 89 Cr App R 17

A police officer seized hold of D and told him that she was arresting him. He dived through a window, dragging her with him as far as the window so that her face was badly cut by the glass. His conviction for wounding with intent to resist arrest (s 18) was quashed because the trial judge directed the jury that D would be guilty if either he foresaw the risk of injury or it would have been obvious to an ordinary prudent man. The Court of Appeal quashed the conviction, holding that the direction was wrong.

Where the ulterior intent for s 18 was an intent to resist arrest, 'maliciously' has same meaning as in *Cunningham*. This means that the prosecution must prove that D realized there was a risk of injury and took that risk.

One unresolved point is what degree of harm does the defendant need to foresee? Does he need to foresee that serious harm or a wound will be caused or does he only need to foresee that some harm will be caused? Under s 20 the test is that the defendant should foresee that some physical harm will be caused. For consistency it seems reasonable that the same test should apply.

12.4 Wound/grievous bodily harm

DC | *JCC v Eisenhower* [1983] 3 All ER 230

V was hit in the eye by a shotgun pellet. This did not penetrate the eye but caused severe bleeding under the surface. As there was no cut, it was held that this was not a wound. The cut must be of the whole skin, so that a scratch is not considered a wound

To constitute a wound, all the external layers of the skin must be broken. Internal bleeding will not suffice for a wound.

HL | *DPP v Smith* [1961] AC 290, (1960) 44 Cr App R 261

D was charged with murder when he drove erratically while a police officer was clinging to his car. The officer was eventually thrown off the car into the path of another vehicle which ran over him causing him fatal injuries. Since the *mens rea* for murder includes an intention to cause grievous bodily harm, one of the issues was the meaning of 'grievous bodily harm'.

Grievous bodily harm should be given its ordinary and natural meaning of 'really serious harm'. GBH does not have to be life threatening, nor does the harm have to have lasting consequences.

Viscount Kilmuir LC
'The words "grievous bodily harm" are to be given their ordinary and natural meaning. "Bodily harm" needs no explanation, and "grievous" means ... really serious...The prosecution does not have to prove that the harm was life-threatening, dangerous or permanent... There is no requirement that the victim should require treatment or that the harm should extend beyond soft tissue damage'.

 CA *Bollom* [2004] 2 Cr App R 6

A 17-month-old child had bruising to her abdomen, both arms and left leg. D was charged with causing grievous bodily harm.

The severity of the injuries should be assessed according to V's age and health. Bruising could amount to grievous bodily harm. Bruising of this severity would be less serious on an adult in full health than on a very young child.

CHAPTER 13

SEXUAL OFFENCES

RAPE

Williams (1923)
Consent induced by fraud as to the nature of the act is not a defence

R (1991)
A man may be prosecuted for raping his wife

SEXUAL OFFENCES

OTHER OFFENCES

H (2005)
(1) Touching can include touching clothing
(2) There is a two-stage approach in deciding whether a touching is sexual under s 78(b)

BIGAMY

Tolson (1889)
Where D has honest and reasonable belief in mistaken facts, then the defence of mistake is available

13.1 Rape

 Williams [1923] 1 KB 340, (1923) 17 Cr App R 56

A choir master had sexual intercourse with a 16-year-old girl after telling her that he was going to perform a procedure that would help her singing. She did not realise it was sexual intercourse. His conviction for rape was upheld.

There is no genuine consent to sexual intercourse when the consent is obtained by fraud.

Elbekkay [1995] Crim LR 163.

 R [1991] 4 All ER 481, (1991) 94 Cr App R 216

See **1.2**.

The common law rule that a man could not rape his wife was abolished. If a wife does not consent to sexual intercourse with her husband then he can be guilty of rape.

13.2 *Mens rea* of rape

Sexual Offences Act 2003, s 1 (the definition of rape)

(a) D intentionally penetrates the vagina, anus or mouth of another person with his penis; and

(b) V does not consent to the penetration; and

(c) D does not reasonably believe that V consents.

This new definition means that *DPP v Morgan* [1975] 2 All ER 411, (1975) 61 Cr App R 136 is no longer relevant to the *mens rea* of rape. *Morgan* allowed a defendant to be judged on his genuine mistaken belief of the facts. It was not necessary that the mistaken belief was reasonable. Element (c) in the new definition reverses this as it includes the requirement that a mistaken belief in consent must be reasonable.

13.3 The Sexual Offences Act 2003

H (2005) 149 SJLB 179, The Times, 8 February 2005

D approached V in the street and said 'Do you fancy a shag?' V ignored him, but D then grabbed the side of her tracksuit bottoms and attempted to pull her towards him. She broke free and ran off. D's conviction for sexual assault under s 3 of the Sexual Offences Act 2003 was upheld.

(1) Touching can include touching clothing.

(2) Section 78(b) creates a two-stage approach in deciding whether a touching is 'sexual'.

13.4 Bigamy

CCR *Tolson* (1889) 23 QBD 168

D believed her husband had drowned when his boat sank at sea. In fact, her husband had jumped ship and was not on board when it sank. Believing that he was dead, D re-married. She was convicted of bigamy.

The defence of mistake is available where D honestly and reasonably held a mistaken belief in facts which would, if true have afforded a defence.

Cave J

'At common law an honest and reasonable belief in the existence of circumstances which, if true, would make the act for which the prisoner is indicted an innocent act has always been held to be a good defence'.

CHAPTER 14

THEFT, ROBBERY AND BURGLARY

APPROPRIATION
Lawrence **(1971)**
There can be an appropriation where V does not genuinely consent to the taking
Gomez **(1993)**
Appropriation is the assumption of any of the rights of an owner
Hinks **(2000)**
Appropriation is a neutral word
There is no differentiation between cases of consent induced by fraud and consent given in any other circumstance

BELONGING TO ANOTHER
Turner (No 2) **(1971)**
Property is regarded as belonging to any person having possession or control
Davidge v Bunnett **(1984)**
Property handed over by another to be retained and dealt with in a particular way belongs to that other
A-G's Ref (No 1 of 1983) **(1984)**
Where property is obtained by a mistake and there is a legal obligation to make restoration to another, then that property is regarded as belonging to that other

THEFT

MENS REA
Ghosh **(1982)**
Two-part test for dishonesty:
(1) is it dishonest by ordinary standard?
(2) if so, did D know it was dishonest by those standards?
DPP v Lavender **(1994)**
Disposal can include 'dealing with' property
Lloyd **(1985)**
Borrowing can be equivalent to an outright taking where the property is kept until the goodness or the value has gone

14.1 Theft

CA | *Lawrence* (1971) 57 Cr App R 64

An Italian student, who had just arrived in England, took a taxi ride. It should have cost 50p, but D took £7 when the student offered his wallet to D to take the correct money for the fare.

There can be an appropriation where V does not genuinely consent to the taking.

HL | *Gomez* [1993] 1 All ER 1

Gomez was the assistant manager of a shop. He persuaded the manager to sell electrical goods worth over £17,000 to an accomplice and to accept payment by two cheques, telling him they were as good as cash. The cheques were stolen and had no value. Gomez was convicted of theft of the goods.

An assumption of any of the rights of an owner is sufficient for an appropriation. There is no need for adverse interference with or usurpation of some right of the owner.

HL | *Hinks*
[2000] 4 All ER 833, [2001] 1 Cr App R 252

D was a 38-year-old woman who had befriended a man of low IQ who was very naïve. He was, however, mentally capable of understanding the concept of ownership and of making a valid gift. D gradually withdrew about £60,000 from his building society account and this money was deposited in D's account. The man also gave D a television set. She was convicted of theft of the money and the TV set.

'Appropriation' is a neutral word. There is no differentiation between cases of consent induced by fraud and consent given in any other circumstance. All situations are appropriation, even where there is a gift.

Although there may be appropriation, there are problems with the other elements of theft in gift situations. Lord Hobhouse dissented because of these problems. He pointed out that that, as a gift transfers the ownership in the goods to the donee at the moment the owner completes the transfer, the property ceased to be 'property belonging to another' unless it could be brought within the situations identified in s 5 of the Theft Act 1968. Also under s6 the donee would not be acting regardless of the donor's rights as the donor has already surrendered his rights.

Oxford v Moss (1978) 68 Cr App R 183

D was a university student who acquired a proof of an examination paper he was due to sit. It was accepted that D did not intend permanently to deprive the university of the piece of paper on which the questions were printed. But he was charged with theft of confidential information (ie the knowledge of the questions). He was found not guilty.

Knowledge of the questions was not intangible property within the definition of s 4 of the Theft Act 1968.

 Kelly and Lindsay [1998] 3 All ER 741

K was a sculptor who asked L, a laboratory assistant at the Royal College of Surgeons, to take body parts from there. K then made casts of the parts. Both were convicted of theft of the body parts.

Body parts, which had acquired 'different attributes' by the application of skill such as dissection or preservation, were capable of being property within the definition in s 4 of the Theft Act 1968. Normally, a dead body is not property under that definition.

Turner (No 2) [1971] 2 All ER 441, (1971) 55 Cr App R 336

D left his car at a garage for repairs. It was agreed that he would pay for the repairs when he collected the car after the repairs had been completed. When the repairs were almost finished the garage left the car parked on the roadway outside their premises. D used a spare key to take the car during the night, without paying for the repairs. D was convicted of theft of the car.

For the purposes of the definition of theft, property is regarded as belonging to any person who has possession or control over it as well as anyone having a proprietary right. This means that the owner of an item can be charged with theft if V has possession or control of it.

 Davidge v Bunnett [1984] Crim LR 297

D was given money by her flatmates to pay the gas bill but instead used it to buy Christmas presents. She was convicted of theft of the money.

Under s 5(3) of the Theft Act 1968 property belongs to the other where it is received from the other under an obligation to retain or deal with it in a particular way.

Klineberg and Marsden [1999] Crim LR 419.

Attorney-General's Reference (No 1 of 1983)
[1984] 3 All ER 369, (1984) 79 Cr App R 288

D's salary was paid into her bank account by transfer. On one occasion her employers mistakenly overpaid her by £74.74. She did not return the money. She was acquitted by the jury of theft but the prosecution sought a ruling on a point of law.

When D gets property by mistake and there is a legal obligation to make restoration, then that property belongs to the other for the purposes of the Theft Act 1968.

Gilks [1972] 3 All ER 280.

CA *Ghosh* [1982] 2 All ER 689, (1982) 75 Cr App R 154

 D was a doctor acting as a locum consultant in a hospital. He claimed fees for an operation he had not carried out. D said that he was not dishonest as he was owed the same amount for consultation fees. The trial judge directed the jury that they must apply their own standards to decide if what he did was dishonest. He was convicted and the Court of Appeal upheld the conviction.

 There is a two-part test for dishonesty:

1 the jury must first of all decide whether according to the ordinary standards of reasonable and honest people what was done was dishonest; if it is then

2 the jury must consider whether the defendant himself must have realised that what he was doing was by those standards dishonest

Lord Lane CJ
'It is dishonest for a defendant to act in a way which he knows ordinary people consider to be dishonest, even if he asserts or genuinely believes that he morally justified in acting as he did. For example, Robin Hood or those ardent anti-vivisectionists who remove animals from vivisection laboratories are acting dishonestly, even though they may consider themselves to be morally justified in doing what they do, because they know that ordinary people would consider these actions to be dishonest'.

DC *DPP v Lavender* [1994] Crim LR 297

D took doors from a council property which was being repaired and used then to replace damaged doors in his girlfriend's council flat. The doors were still in the possession of the council but had been transferred without permission from one council property to another. D was convicted of theft.

Disposal can include 'dealing with' property. So if D intended to treat the doors as his own, regardless of the rights of the council, then s 6 of the Theft Act 1968 is satisfied.

Lloyd [1985] 2 All ER 661, (1986) 81 Cr App R 182

The projectionist at a local cinema gave D a film that was showing at the cinema so that D could make an illegal copy. D returned the film in time for the next screening at the cinema. His conviction for theft was quashed because, by returning the film in its original state, it was not possible to prove an intention to permanently deprive.

Borrowing is not theft unless it is for a period and in circumstances making it equivalent to an outright taking or disposal. This can occur where property is kept until the goodness or the value has gone.

Lord Lane CJ
'[Section 6(1)] is intended to make clear that a mere borrowing is never enough to constitute the necessary guilty mind unless the intention is to return the "thing" in such a changed state that it can truly be said that all its goodness or virtue has gone'.

> **ROBBERY**
> *Robinson* **(1977)**
> All the elements of theft must be present for the offence of robbery to be committed
> *Clouden* **(1987)**
> Only minimal force is needed
> *Hale* **(1978)**
> Theft is a continuing act for the purposes of robbery. Force used to escape is still at the time of the theft and in order to steal

ROBBERY AND BURGLARY

> **BURGLARY**
> *Collins* **(1972)**
> (1) D must know he is a trespasser or be reckless as that fact
> (2) The entry must be 'effective and substantial'
> *Brown* **(1985)**
> The entry must be 'effective': there is no need for it to be substantial
> *Ryan* **(1996)**
> The entry need not be effective as to the ulterior offence
> *Walkington* **(1979)**
> Any clearly defined area of a building can be 'part of a building'
> *Smith and Jones* **(1976)**
> If D goes beyond the permission given for entry, he may become a trespasser

14.2 Robbery

CA *Robinson* **[1977] Crim LR 173**

D was owed £7 by V's wife. D threatened V. During a struggle V dropped a £5 note and D took it. D's conviction for robbery was quashed because the trial judge had wrongly directed the jury that D had honestly to believe he was entitled to get the money in that way.

(1) There must be a completed theft for there to be robbery.
(2) If D had a genuine belief that he had a right in law to the money, then his actions are not dishonest under s 2(1)(a) of the Theft Act 1968.

Clouden [1987] Crim LR 56

D wrenched a shopping basket from V's hand. He was convicted of robbery. The Court of Appeal upheld his conviction as the trial judge had been right to leave the question of whether D had used force on a person to the jury.

'Force' is an ordinary word and it is for the jury to decide if force has been used.

The Criminal Law Revision Committee who put forward the draft Bill for the Theft Act 1978 stated that they would 'not regard mere snatching of property, such as a handbag, from an unresisting owner as using force for the purpose of the definition [of robbery]'. The courts have ignored this in their decisions on force.

Dawson and James (1976) 64 Cr App R 170.

CA *Hale* (1978) 68 Cr App R 415

Two defendants forced their way into V's house. D1 put his hand over V's mouth to stop her screaming while D2 went upstairs and took a jewellery box. Before they left the house they tied up V and gagged her. Their convictions for burglary were upheld.

For the purposes of robbery theft is a continuous act. Appropriation does not cease when D picks up an item. It is open to the jury to decide if the theft is still ongoing at the point when force is used.

The tying up of V was considered as force 'at the time' of the theft. Although this does seem a sensible interpretation, it is not consistent with the court's decision in *Gomez* (1993) (see **12.1**). In *Gomez*, it was held that the point of appropriation is when D first does an act assuming the right of an owner. At this point the theft is completed.

 Lockley [1995] Crim LR 656.

14.3 Burglary

CA *Collins* [1972] 2 All ER 1105, (1972) 56 Cr App R 554

D climbed a ladder to an open window. He saw a naked girl asleep in bed. He then went down the ladder, took off all his clothes except for his socks and climbed back. As he was on the window sill outside the room, she woke up, thought he was her boyfriend and helped him into the room where they had sex. D's conviction for burglary was

> quashed as it could not be proved that he was a trespasser at the time of entry.
>
>
>
> (1) There must be an effective and substantial entry as a trespasser for D to be liable for burglary.
> (2) To be a trespasser D must enter either knowing he is a trespasser, or being reckless as to whether or not he has consent to enter the premises.

CA *Brown* [1985] Crim LR 212

D was leaning in through a shop window, rummaging through goods. His feet and lower part of his body were outside the shop. He was convicted of burglary.

The word 'substantial' used by the Court of Appeal in *Collins* (1973) does not materially assist the definition of entry. It is sufficient if the entry is effective

CA *Ryan* [1996] Crim LR 320

D was trapped when trying to get through a window into a house. His head and right arm were inside the house but the rest of his body was outside. The fire brigade had to be called to release him. The Court of Appeal upheld his conviction for burglary.

There need only be proof of entry. The entry does not have to be effective to commit the ulterior offence.

There is no definition of 'entry' in the Theft Act 1968. The wording of 'effective and substantial entry' was first used in *Collins*. However, *Brown* and *Ryan* have moved away from that test put forward in *Collins*.

CA *Walkington* [1979] 2 All ER 716, (1979) 63 Cr App R 427

D went into a counter area in a shop and opened a till. D's conviction for burglary under s 9(1)(a) was upheld as he had entered part of a building as a trespasser.

D can be a trespasser in part of a building, even though he has permission to be in the rest of the building.

CA *Smith and Jones* [1976] 3 All ER 54, (1976) 63 Cr App Rep 47

Smith and his friend went to Smith's father's house and took two television sets without the father's knowledge or permission. The father said his son had a general permission to enter. Their convictions for burglary were upheld as they had gone beyond the permission given them to enter.

Entering a building with intent to steal removes any permission that normally exists for D to enter that building. D becomes a trespasser if he knowingly enters in excess of the permission that has been given to him to enter, or when he is reckless whether he is entering in excess of the permission.

CHAPTER 15

OTHER OFFENCES UNDER THE THEFT ACTS

TAKING A CONVEYANCE WITHOUT CONSENT
Bogacki (1973)
There must be some movement of the vehicle for a taking
McKnight v Davies (1974)
If D goes beyond the permission for use, he can be guilty of this offence
Marsh (1997)
For aggravated-vehicle taking there is no need for D to be at fault in respect of any injury or damage done

TAKING A CONVEYANCE WITHOUT CONSENT and HANDLING

HANDLING
A-G's Ref (No 1 of 1974) (1974)
The goods must be stolen goods: if they have been reduced into police possession they may no longer be stolen
Pitchley (1972)
Retention means 'keep possession of, not lose, continue to have'
Kanwar (1982)
Assisting in retention can include representations such as lying about the origin of goods

15.1 Taking without consent

CA *Bogacki* [1973] 2 All ER 864, (1973) 57 Cr App R 593

Three defendants had got onto a bus in a depot and tried, unsuccessfully, to start it. The Court of Appeal quashed their conviction for taking without consent as there was no 'taking'.

There must be unauthorised taking possession or control of the vehicle by D, adverse to the rights of the true owner, coupled with some movement of the vehicle. The movement need only be very small.

DC *McKnight v Davies* [1974] RTR 4, [1974] Crim LR 62

D was a lorry driver who had not returned a lorry at the end of his working day but had used it for his own purposes. He then returned it in the early hours of the following morning. His conviction for an offence under s 12 of the Theft Act 1968 was upheld.

Where the owner has given consent for D to use the conveyance for a particular purpose, D can be guilty of taking without consent if he goes beyond the permission given.

CA *Marsh* [1997] 1 Cr App R 67

D was driving, when a pedestrian ran out in front of a car D had taken and was slightly injured. D was not to blame for the incident. D's conviction for aggravated vehicle-taking was upheld.

For aggravated vehicle-taking, the prosecution needs to prove only that D committed the basic offence of taking and that one of the prohibited events then occurred. There is no need to prove fault in respect of the prohibited happenings, ie injury owing to the driving, damage to other property owing to the driving or damage to the vehicle.

15.2 Handling

 Attorney-General's Reference (No 1 of 1974)
[1974] 2 All ER 899

A police officer suspected that goods in the back of a parked car were stolen, so he removed the rotor arm of the car to prevent it being driven away and kept watch. When D returned to the car the officer arrested him because he could not give a satisfactory explanation. D was acquitted of handling stolen goods. The point at issue was whether the goods were still stolen goods or whether they had been taken into police possession.

The goods must be stolen goods at the time of the handling. If the goods have been restored to their original owner or taken into police possession, they are no longer stolen goods. This will depend on the specific facts of each case.

CA *Pitchley* (1972) 57 Cr App R 30

D was given £150 in cash by his son who asked him to take care of it for him. D put the money into his Post Office savings account. At the time of receiving the money D was not aware that it was stolen. Two days later D found out that it was stolen. He left the money in the account. He was convicted of handling. By leaving the money in the account he had retained it on behalf of another person.

'Retention' in s 24 of the Theft Act 1968 means 'keep possession of, not lose, continue to have'.

 CA *Kanwar* [1982] 2 All ER 528, (1982) 75 Cr App R 87

D's husband had used stolen goods to furnish their home. D was aware that the items were stolen. When the police called and made inquiries about them, she gave untrue answers about where the items had come from.

Verbal representations, whether oral or in writing, for the purpose of concealing the identity of stolen goods may, if made dishonestly and for the benefit of another, amount to handling stolen goods by assisting in their retention.

> **GOING EQUIPPED**
> *Doukas* (1978)
> The items must be for use in an offence
> *Ellames* (1974)
> 'For use' applies only to future offences: there is no offence if D has completed the offence

> **MAKING OFF WITHOUT PAYMENT**
> *Vincent* (2001)
> It has to be proved that payment 'on the spot' was required or expected
> *Allen* (1985)
> There must an intention to evade payment altogether

GOING EQUIPPED, BLACKMAIL and MAKING OFF WITHOUT PAYMENT

> **BLACKMAIL**
> *Treacy* (1971)
> The offence is commited when the demand is made
> *Clear* (1968)
> It is not necessary to prove that V was actually intimidated by the threats
> *Garwood* (1987)
> A threat which would not affect a normal person can be menaces if D was aware of the likely effect it would have on the specific victim
> *Bevans* (1988)
> Any property can be the subject of the 'gain' or 'loss'

15.3 Going equipped

 Doukas [1978] 1 All ER 1061, (1978) 66 Cr App R 228

D was a wine waiter in a hotel. He took bottles of wine into the hotel intending to sell them to people dining at the hotel so that he could pocket the money. The main point on appeal was whether they were for use in a s 15 offence of obtaining money by deception. His conviction was upheld.

There was a potential offence of obtaining money by deception as diners in the hotel would refuse to have the wine if they knew that it was brought in by D for his own profit. They were being deceived.

CA *Ellames* [1974] 3 All ER 130

D was stopped by the police and found to have with him masks, guns and gloves which had been used in a robbery. D was trying to get rid of these. His conviction was quashed as he did not have the article 'for use' as the robbery was in the past.

The 'for use' applies only to future offences. Where D has already committed the offence and does not intend to commit further offences with the items, there is no offence of going equipped.

15.4 Making off without payment

CA *Vincent* [2001] EWCA Crim 295, [2001] Cr App R 150

D had stayed at two hotels and not paid his bills. He said that he had arranged with the proprietors of each to pay when he could, so payment on the spot was not required or expected.

His conviction was quashed.

It has to be proved that payment 'on the spot' was required or expected. If there is an agreement to defer payment then payment 'on the spot' is not required and there is no offence under s 3.

HL *Allen* **[1985] 2 All ER 64, (1985) 81 Cr App R 200**

D owed £1,286 for his stay at a hotel. He left without paying, but his defence was that he genuinely intended to pay in the near future as he was expecting to receive sufficient money to cover the bill. His conviction was quashed.

The phrase 'and with intent to avoid payment of the amount due' means there must an intention to evade payment altogether. Merely intending to delay or defer payment is not sufficient for the *mens rea* of s 3.

15.5 Blackmail

HL *Treacy* **[1971] 1 All ER 110, (1971) 55 Cr App R 113**

D posted a letter containing a demand with menaces in England to someone in Germany.

Making the demand is the *actus reus* of the offence. The

demand does not have to be received by the victim. When a demand is sent through the post the demand is considered made at the point the letter is posted.

CA *Clear* [1968] 1 All ER 74, (1968) 52 Cr App R 58

D was an employee of a company who were making a civil claim against their insurers over a stolen lorry. D was required to give evidence. He demanded money from the managing director on the threat that he would give evidence that would be unfavourable to the company.

The menace must be of such a nature and extent that the mind of an ordinary person of ordinary courage and firmness might be influenced or made apprehensive by it so as to unwillingly accede to the demand. It is not necessary to prove that the intended victim of the demand was himself alarmed by it.

CA *Garwood* [1987] 1 All ER 1032, (1987) 85 Cr App R 85

D accused V of 'doing over' D's house and demanded money and jewellery 'to make it quits'. V was unusually timid and acceded to the demand.

A threat which would not affect a normal person can be menaces if D was aware of the likely effect it would have on the specific victim.

Harry [1974] Crim LR 32.

CA ***Bevans* [1988] Crim LR 236, (1988) 87 Cr App R 64**

D suffered from osteo–arthritis which caused him severe pain. He called a doctor to his house and then pointed a gun at the doctor and demanded a morphine injection for pain relief. His conviction for blackmail was upheld.

The drug involved in the injection was property under s 34 of the Theft Act 1968 which specifies that the gain or loss must be in money or other property.

DECEPTION OFFENCES

DECEPTION
MPC v Charles **(1976)**
(1) presenting a cheque is a
    representation that it will be met
(2) the use of a cheque card to back a
    cheque is a representation that D
    has bank's authority
Lambie **(1981)**
Use of a credit card is a representation
that D has authority of bank to use it
DPP v Ray **(1973)**
Silence can be conduct for the purposes
of deception
Firth **(1990)**
Failure to disclose information where D is
under a duty to do so is deception

DECEPTION OFFENCES

THEFT ACT 1978
Sofroniou **(2003)**
A common understanding
that the benefit will be
paid for is sufficient
Silbartie **(1983)**
Use of an invalid ticket is
a representation and can
give liability under
s 2(1)(c)

OBTAINING
Collis-Smith **(1971)**
The deception must be made
before the obtaining
Laverty **(1970)**
A deception about a fact
which does not act on V's
mind has not caused the
obtaining

NOTE The law will be changed by the Fraud Bill 2005. The
cases in this chapter are decisions on deception offences in the
Theft Act 1968 and the Theft Act 1978. Included under
comments on the cases are the effects that the Fraud Bill
will have.

16.1 Deception

 HL *Metropolitan Police Commissioner v Charles*
[1976] 3 All ER 112, (1976) 63 Cr App R 252

D had a bank account and a cheque card for it which
guaranteed that any cheques he wrote up to £30 would be
honoured by the bank. D wrote out 25 cheques for £30 in
order to buy gaming chips and backed each cheque with the
cheque card. He knew that he did not have enough money in
his account to meet the cheques and that the amount would
exceed his overdraft limit.

(1) There is an implied representation when a person draws a
    cheque that it will be met.
(2) By using a cheque card to back a cheque, D is representing
    that he has actual authority from the bank to make a
    contract with the payee on the bank's behalf that it will
    honour the cheque on presentment for payment.

 HL *Lambie* [1981] 2 All ER 776, (1981) 73 Cr App R 294

D had exceeded her credit card limit and the bank which had
issued the card wrote, asking her to return the card. She agreed
that she would return the card, but did not do so. After this
she purchased goods using the card.

The same principle in *Lambie* applies to cheque cards and
credit cards. D is representing that he has the authority of the
issuing bank to use the credit card.

Gilmartin [1983] QB 953.

16.2 Silence as deception

HL *DPP v Ray* [1973] 3 All ER 131, (1973) 58 Cr App R 130

D went to a restaurant with three friends. He did not have enough money to pay for a meal but one of his friends agreed to lend him enough to pay for the meal. After eating the meal they all decided not to pay for it and ran out of the restaurant without paying.

Silence can be conduct for the purposes of deception where a true representation (that he would pay for the meal) becomes false when the representation ceases to be true (as when D he decides not to pay).

The Fraud Bill 2005 will introduce an offence of fraud by failing to disclose information. This will be committed where a person:

(a) dishonestly fails to disclose information which he is under a legal duty to disclose; and
(b) intends by failing to disclose the information –
   (i) to make a gain for himself or another, or
   (ii) to cause loss to another or to expose another to the risk of loss.

It seems that *Ray* would not come under this new offence as D was not under a legal duty to disclose information. However, a person who acts as Ray did could be charged with the offence of making off without payment.

 Rai [2000] Crim LR 192, [2000] 1 Cr App R 349

D applied for a grant from the local council towards installing a downstairs bathroom for his elderly mother. Two days after the council had approved the grant, D's mother died. D carried on with the improvement and did not tell the local council of his mother's death.

Silence can be conduct for the purposes of deception where circumstances have changed and the defendant does not inform the other person of the change.

 Firth [1990] Crim LR 326, (1989) 91 Cr App R 217

D was a doctor who failed to inform the NHS hospital where he worked that some of the patients he had seen there were private patients. This meant that he avoided paying charges to the hospital for the private patients.

Silence can be deception where D is under a duty to disclose information and fails to do so.

These cases on silence as deception mean that D can be liable for an omission, a failure to give information. Both situations are likely to be an offence under the new offence of fraud by failing to disclose information.

16.3 Obtaining

CA *Collis-Smith* [1971] Crim LR 716

D filled up his car with petrol. This meant that at that moment ownership of the petrol had passed to him. He then falsely claimed that his company would pay for the petrol. His conviction under s 15 was quashed as the petrol had not been obtained by his deception.

The deception must be the cause of the obtaining.

This gap in the law was covered by the offence of evading a liability by deception under s 2 of the 1978 Theft Act. However, the Fraud Bill 2005 makes proposes the offence of fraud by false representation which will be committed if D:

(a) dishonestly makes a false representation, and
(b) intends, by making the false representation –
   (i) to make a gain for himself or another, or
   (ii) to cause loss to another or to expose another to the risk of loss.

Under this it will not be necessary to prove that anything was obtained.

CA *Laverty* [1970] 3 All ER 432, (1971) 54 Cr App R 495

D changed the registration number plates and the chassis number on a car and sold the car to P. The changing of the numbers was a representation that the car was the original car to which these numbers had been allocated. D's conviction was quashed because there was no evidence that the false numbers had induced the sale.

Where the deception is about a matter which is irrelevant to V then it does not cause the obtaining and so no offence is committed.

This would be an offence under the proposed offence of fraud by false representation. There will be no need to prove that the false representation was the cause of the obtaining.

16.4 Theft Act 1978 offences

 Sofroniou [2003] EWCA Crim 3681

D operated two bank accounts under false names. He arranged for loans from both banks and became overdrawn on the accounts. He also applied for a credit card and exceeded the credit limit paced on the card. His convictions under s 1 of the Theft Act 1978 were upheld. The issue was whether under s 1(2) there was an 'understanding that the benefit has been or will be paid for'.

There is no need for a specific agreement that the benefit will be paid for. A common understanding that there will be payment for a service is sufficient, such as the common understanding that loans and overdrafts are paid for.

This situation would presumably be covered by the proposed offence of fraud by false representation.

CA *Sibartie* **[1983] Crim LR 470**

D had valid tickets for the beginning and end of his journey but not for the middle part of the journey. On changing trains he flashed an invalid season ticket so quickly that the ticket inspector could not see what was on it. He was convicted of attempted evasion of a liability contrary to s 2(1)(c) of the Theft Act 1978.

(1) The showing of the ticket was a representation that D had a valid ticket. This, if it had succeeded, would have exempted him from paying the extra fare and was an offence under s 2(1)(c).
(2) It is also possible that this conduct could amount to the offence of evasion of a liability under s 2(1)(b).

The Fraud Bill 2005 includes an offence of obtaining services dishonestly. Under the Bill a person obtains services if –

(a) they are made available on the basis that payment has been or will be made for or in respect of them;
(b) he obtains them without any payment having been made or without payment in full being made;
(c) when he obtains them he knows –
    (i)   that they are being made available on the basis of payment, or
    (ii) that they might be, but intends that payment will not be made.

CHAPTER 17

CRIMINAL DAMAGE

DAMAGE
Hardman v Chief Constable of Avon **(1986)**
Roe v Kingerlee **(1986)** The damage does not need to be permanent. The expense and trouble of removing it can be considered

ENDANGERING LIFE
Steer **(1987)** The danger must come from the damage and not from the act

CRIMINAL DAMAGE

MENS REA
G and another **(2003)** D must have been aware of the risk of damage occurring: the test is subjective

s 5 DEFENCES
Kelleher **(2003)**
To have a defence under s 5 (b)(2) the act of damage must be done from the immediate protection of property of another
Jaggard v Dickinson **(1980)**
s 5(3) requires the court to consider D's actual state of mind: intoxication is irrelevant

17.1 Damage

Cr
Ct

Hardman v Chief Constable of Avon and Somerset Constabulary [1986] Crim LR 330

CND protesters, to mark the 40th anniversary of the dropping of the atomic bomb on Hiroshima, painted silhouettes on the pavement with water soluble paint. The local council paid to have the paintings removed with water jets. D argued that it would have washed away with rain. They were convicted.

Damage does not have to be permanent. The mischief done to property and the expense and trouble of removing it can be considered.

DC

Roe v Kingerlee [1986] Crim LR 735

D had smeared mud on the walls of a police cell. It cost £7 to have it cleaned off.

It was held that this could be damage even though it was not permanent.

17.2 *Mens rea*

HL *G and another* [2003] UKHL 50

Two boys aged 11 and 12 years set fire to some bundles of newspapers in a shop yard. They threw the burning papers under a large wheelie bin and left the yard. The bin caught fire; this spread to the shop and other buildings causing about £1 million damage. The boys were convicted under both s 1 and s 3 of the Criminal Damage Act 1971. On appeal, the House of Lords quashed their conviction.

Recklessness for the purposes of the *mens rea* of criminal damage means the D must have been aware of the risk of damage occurring. it is a subjective test.

Lord Bingham (quoting the Draft Criminal Code):

'A person acts recklessly within the meaning of section 1 of the Criminal Damage Act 1971 with respect to –

(i) a circumstance when he is aware of a risk that it exists or will exist;

(ii) a result when he is aware of a risk that it will occur;

and it is in the circumstances known to him, unreasonable to take the risk'.

This decision overruled *Caldwell* [1981] 1 All ER 961. The House of Lords held that in *Caldwell* the Law Lords had 'adopted an interpretation of section 1 of the 1971 Act which was beyond the range of feasible meanings'. They emphasised that when the Criminal Damage Act was drafted the Law Commission had not intended that the *mens rea* for the offence be changed. They had merely replaced the old-fashioned word of 'maliciously' used in previous Acts with the phrase 'intending or being reckless'.

17.3 Section 5 defences

CA | *Kelleher* [2003] EWCA Crim 3525

D had strong and genuine concerns that the policies of the USA and UK were leading towards the eventual destruction of the world. He believed that Lady Thatcher was one of those responsible for the state of affairs. He knocked off the head of a statue of Lady Thatcher. The trial judge ruled as a matter of law that the defence of lawful excuse under s 5(2)(b) of the Criminal Damage Act 1971 was not available. D's conviction was upheld.

The act of damage must be done in order to protect property belonging to another.

*   *Blake v DPP* [1993] Crim LR 586;
*   *Hill* (1988).

Jaggard v Dickinson [1980] 3 All ER 716

D, who was drunk, went to what she thought was a friend's house. There was no-one in and so she broke a window to get in as she correctly believed her friend would consent to this. In fact, she broke into the wrong house.

Section 5(3) requires the court to consider D's actual state of belief. It is irrelevant that D was intoxicated.

17.4 Endangering life

 Steer [1987] 2 All ER 833

D fired three shots at the home of his former business partner, causing damage to the house. The Court of Appeal quashed his conviction as they held that the danger came from the shots, not from any damage done to the house through those shots.

The danger to life for an offence under s 1(2) must come from the damage itself.

Webster and Warwick [1995] 2 All ER 168.

PUBLIC ORDER OFFENCES

AFFRAY
Dixon (1993)
An act such as encouraging a dog to attack can be conduct for the purposes of affray
Davison (1992)
(1) An affray can be committed on private property
(2) It is not necessary for a person of reasonable firmness to have been at the scene
I, M and H v DPP (2001)
(1) Carrying dangerous weapons can be the threat of unlawful violence for affray
(2) There must be someone present at the scene who was threatened with unlawful violence for affray

---

INSULTING BEHAVIOUR
Brutus v Cozens (1972)
Whether words, behaviour or writing etc are 'threatening, abusive or insulting' under s 5 is a question of fact

---

18.1 Affray

CA *Dixon* [1993] Crim LR 579

D ran away from the police following a domestic incident. The officers cornered him and he encouraged his dog to attack them. Two officers were bitten. D's conviction for affray was upheld.

'An act such as encouraging a dog to attack can be conduct for the purpose of affray'.

CA *Davison* **[1992] Crim LR 31**

The police were called to a domestic incident. D threatened a police officer with an eight-inch knife. D's conviction for affray was upheld.

(1) An affray can be committed on private property.
(2) It is not necessary for a person of reasonable firmness to have been at the scene. The test was whether a person of reasonable firmness would have feared for his safety, not whether the police officer actually did fear for his personal safety.

HL *I, M and H v DPP* **[2001] UKHL 10, [2001] 2 Cr App R 216**

The defendants had armed themselves with petrol bombs to use against a rival gang. The police arrived before the Ds met up with the rival gang. The moment the police arrived the Ds threw the petrol bombs away and dispersed. Their convictions for affray were quashed by the House of Lords.

(1) The carrying of dangerous weapons such as petrol bombs could constitute the threat of unlawful violence for the offence of affray. This was true whether or not the weapons were brandished.
(2) There must be someone present at the scene who was threatened with unlawful violence for the offence of affray to be committed.

18.2 Threatening, abusive or insulting behaviour

Brutus v Cozens [1972] 2 All ER 1297, (1972) 56 Cr App R 799

D made a protest about apartheid by running on to the court, blowing a whistle and distributing leaflets during a Wimbledon tennis match. He was acquitted of an offence under s 5 of the Public Order Act 1936. This offence has since been abolished but the words used in it of 'threatening, abusive or insulting' are contained in s 4 of the 1986 Public Order Act.

'It is a question of fact whether the words, behaviour or writing etc are "threatening, abusive or insulting". In *Brutus* the House of Lords held that the magistrates' finding of fact that D's behaviour was not "threatening, abusive or insulting" was not unreasonable and could not be challenged'.

INDEX